WHY CHILDREN MAKE UP STORIES

A Practical Guide to Help Adults Recognize the Underlying Reasons Children Make Up Stories

Susan Louise Peterson

International Scholars Publications
San Francisco - London - Bethesda
1999

Library of Congress Cataloging-in-Publication Data

Peterson, Susan Louise, 1980—
    Why children make up stories: a practical guide to help adults recognize the underlying reasons children make up stories/ Susan Louise Peterson.

        p. cm.
    Includes bibliographical references and index.
        ISBN 1-57309-381-5 (hardcover ; alk.paper) ISBN 1-57309-382-3 (alk. paper)
    1. Interpersonal communication in children. 2. Children and adults. I. Title.
    BF723.C57P47   1999
    155.4'136—dc21   99-10373
                                                                    CIP

Editorial Inquiries:
International Scholars Publications
7831 Woodmont Avenue, #345
Bethesda, MD 20814
website: www.interscholars.com
To order: (800) 55-PUBLISH

Disclaimer
The names have been changed in the book
to protect the identity of the individuals.

WHY CHILDREN MAKE UP STORIES

A Practical Guide to Help Adults Recognize the Underlying Reasons Children Make Up Stories

Susan Louise Peterson

FOREWORD

Social workers, psychologists, school personnel, and law enforcement often find themselves frustrated when questioning children about an incident. Whether it is an abuse or neglect situation or involvement in a criminal act, a child's testimony rarely holds up in a court of law.

Dr. Susan Louise Peterson's new book *Why Children Make Up Stories* is an informative accumulation of actual incidents with thoughtful analysis about what is probably going through a child's mind.

With over twenty years as a social worker and educator, I highly recommend this well-written, easy to read and understand book to all professionals who work with children. Professionals will be better able to advocate for children if they know how to ask appropriate questions and understand why certain questions solicit confusing responses. Often time, we adults do not stop to understand the developmental level of the child we are interacting with, but approach them through our adult eyes. This book helps to sensitize adults to the many influences children are facing when the interaction occurs. Parents and grandparents may find this book helpful in nurturing relationships with young children.

Dr. Peterson's list of 100 cautions in examining children's stories should be mandatory training for professionals.

Alicia Smalley, MSW, Director of Field Instruction
University of Nevada Reno, School of Social Work
President, NASW, Nevada Chapter

FOREWORD

Shortly after young children begin to get a firm grasp on spoken language, they begin to tell stories to defend, explain and enhance their own behavior. These stories have one thing in common, the main character is the child who tells the story. Those who work with young children need both courage and insight to deal with these one-dimensional stories. One needs courage to enter into this "looking-glass" world with children while maintaining a balanced adult view of reality. Insight is necessary for recognizing the part of the child's world that is fantasy. Dr. Peterson's book, *Why Children Make Up Stories*, is a courageous anecdotal record of her experiences with children who try to mold the world about them to fit their own immediate needs. She expects the reader to muster the courage to ask a child if the story is a "real" one or a "pretend" one. She illustrates very vividly the pitfalls that adults often encounter when listening to children's accounts of events and phenomena. Anyone who deals with young children can benefit from the insights provided by Dr. Peterson, not only to avoid difficulty, but also to better understand what children are trying to communicate to them. We owe it to children to confront their misunderstandings of reality and help shape them into authentic satisfying life experiences. No child should suffer the burden of having to live up to his or her own story in which the main character is always right.

B.D. Whetstone, Ph.D.
Professor of Education
Birmingham-Southern College, Birmingham, Alabama

To Alan

TABLE OF CONTENTS

PREFACE

I came up with an idea to write this book partly out of the frustration I faced being a teacher in the public schools. Over years of teaching, I have been questioned (like many teachers), by parents and administrators regarding things a child has said or misinterpreted. It was not long after entering the teaching profession that I became very conscientious about what I said to children and how I responded to the things they told me. I began to spend more time clarifying and questioning the things they told me, rather than brushing over them as I had done during my first years of teaching. With each passing year I found the things a child said became more believable by parents or others. Things a child said twenty years ago were rarely questioned or used as a threat to sue a teacher or other child specialists. Times have changed so that even the slightest statement from a child might be taken out of context and escalated into an exaggerated situation.

This book seeks to grasp the reality of why children make up stories. I have spent hundreds of hours observing and analyzing children's stories and statements. I am concerned with stories children make up and how our world views and distorts much of the information. I wrote this book to assist educators, social workers, psychologists, counselors, child and family life specialists, attorneys, law enforcement officers, parents, and other professionals who explore the world of children's stories. It is my intention to discover some of the hidden meanings and confusion related to their stories.

ACKNOWLEDGMENTS

I would like to thank the following people for their help with the book:

Alicia Smalley, from the University of Nevada-Reno, for giving a social work perspective in the foreword of the book.

B.D. Whetstone, for his insight into the world of children. His ability to understand young children and their behavior is skillful and intuitive.

Dr. Robert West, for his continued feedback and willingness to work with me on book projects.

Alan Peterson, for his patience and support in the manuscript preparation.

My parents, Mary and Vernon, for spending hours listening to my childhood stories.

CHAPTER ONE

THE REALITY OF CHILDREN MAKING UP STORIES

Years ago when a child told a far-fetched story, it was thought as being cute and creative. The child was noticed for being very imaginative and having lots of potential for a great future. With an imagination so vivid, the parents would wonder if the child would someday be a great artist, writer or inventor. Times were different back then. Parents would laugh at those silly stories the children were telling and the innocence of the children. There were times in the past when our country believed in the simple idea of closing a deal with a handshake rather than with a lengthy contract. Getting a divorce meant simply living apart from one another and choosing to live a single lifestyle again. As the American society became "lawsuit happy," children were pulled into legal battles and the innocence of their stories turned into major warfare.

Suddenly, everything a child said became "believable" and could be something used against someone else. Children's made up stories can be taken out of context, and parents can use the stories against each other in battles for legal custody. Children's stories began to be issues of attack, justification and support for or against parents no matter how innocent or harmless the actual story was from the child's perspective.

A teacher's or administrator's credibility and professionalism is called into question when having to address these made up stories. A young child goes home and tells a story to his or her parents. The parent is at the school the next day confronting the teacher and administrator with accusations based upon the made up story. I remember going to my administrator one day to discuss a false accusation a parent was making against me based on a young boy's made up story. The first question the principal asked me, "Was there any other witnesses in the classroom to back your side of the situation?" I promptly told him the incident never took place so there was nothing to witness and my paraprofessional or teacher's aide would back up my statements. The principal told me I was lucky to have another person witness or support my side of the situation. He also told me that this type of thing happens often and he had received four complaints that week of what he considered made up stories against teachers. I am amazed some parents are so gullible as to believe everything their children tell them. I began to wonder if parents were just looking for a reason to sue a teacher, administrator or school district for money.

It is even getting to the point in public schools where a teacher will get together with another teacher or aide when discussing children's concerns with parents. It is kind of like having a third party to witness the interaction as the parent accuses the teacher of an action based on something the child has told him or her. The teacher then has to explain and rationalize with parents why the child made up a story or became confused by details of what happened in class.

The problem in American society is that many professionals are in positions of having to make judgment calls on the believability of these children's stories. Social workers, law enforcement officers, psychologists, counselors, child protective officers, family life specialists, lawyers, doctors, teachers, administrators, judges and juries are in positions of deciding if children's stories are reality or fantasy, fact or fiction, or an array of distorted details. Let me not downplay that some children do tell the truth and re-count actual details of abuse and awful things that have happened to them. My point in writing this book is that parents and professionals must use caution in interpreting the reality, reasons and substance of a story that a child is telling. Outstanding teachers have lost jobs and left the teaching profession over made up stories. Parents have lost custody of their children based on the confusing details of a child's story. Children can be taken from their home environments based on a social worker's or child protective specialist's observation and report of a child's story. Day care centers are cited and closed on alleged charges of abuse based on questionable aspects of the stories children tell. Lives of parents, grandparents, relatives and children are hurt, torn apart, and in some cases destroyed by the misunderstandings found in the stories children have imagined, fantasized and made up for various reasons.

If you think I sound as if I am blaming the children for making up stories that have destroyed families and people, you are wrong. I am blaming society for not letting kids be kids, and for misinterpreting things children say by turning their innocent, imagined and confusing stories into believable incidents. My goal in writing this book is to explore why children make up stories. My observations come from having a background in education, sociology, human relations and family studies. I have seen numerous incidents over my years of experience where children have made-up stories and confused the details of events. As I examined these made up stories and accounts, I found that there were five underlying reasons that children make up stories, events and incidents. Of course, the obvious explanation for why children make up stories is that they are imaginative, desire attention, or lie and deceive to impress others. These three elements are included and addressed numerous times in the book as the five underlying reasons are discussed. The following list is a brief summary of these five underlying reasons:

1. LACK OF REAL LIFE EXPERIENCES

One of the most obvious reasons that children make up stories is they have not had enough real life experiences to understand and validate their ideas. They know about some things, but their lack of experience causes them to have an unclear picture of the actual situation they are describing and telling to others. I have noticed this on numerous occasions when I would teach a career unit to elementary students in an at-risk school. The students had a perception that police officers were bad people. Yet I know their stories and ideas are based on their negative life experiences. They told me how the police took away their parents in a police car or that mom was in jail for taking something from a store. The police took away someone they loved so that made all police officers bad people in their eyes. As these children develop more positive life experiences they gain a more realistic view of the role of police officers in our society. Stories and ideas they share about police officers are often distorted until a positive learning experience occurs.

Some children who lack real life experiences will imitate or repeat other people's stories as if the story or idea was their own. I remember having my students each tell a holiday story during December. I gave an example of a holiday story and told the students about how my family would drive around in our car looking at Christmas lights, and then we would open our presents. At least five other students told the same story as I did, even though I know some of them did not even own a car.

In another language activity, I had students come to tell the class about their favorite food. The first student that came forward to speak was a little boy who had eaten out and had many experiences eating at seafood buffets. He told the class his favorite food to eat was crab legs. I knew that most of the other students in the class did not really know what he was talking about when he told of his experience. However, this did not change the fact that six other kids told the class their favorite food was (you guessed it) crab legs.

The same principle applies when a young child gets hurt on the playground and runs to the teacher with a scratched knee. The teacher gives the child a Band-Aid and a few kind words and the student feels better. Before long, three other students run to the teacher to show the scratches they have and explain how they need a Band-Aid just like the other student. The students have not had enough real life experiences and accidents to know what justifies a Band-Aid or medicine. They also repeat stories based on what parents say to them. A child constantly begging for an aspirin for his headache may not really have a headache, but knows of the experience by observing parents.

I have also seen students hurt on an emotional level because they expect another student's experience to be their own. For instance, Josh's parents brought a cake to celebrate his birthday at school. The other students then start telling me about the big party they were going to have on their upcoming birthdays. When the party does not occur that they have imagined and visualized, they are hurt by the reality of this life experience.

Many children's stories are sincere, but they lack real life experiences. They truly believe the stories they are telling are the truth. Perhaps, this is why the story the child is telling sounds "believable" to some people. It is important for adults to look carefully and observe what childhood experiences are the foundation or base of the story. A child repeating someone else's story can tell a story with such determination and sincerity that it sounds as if the events in the story really happened to him or her. A person observing the child may not understand the child is making something up because of a lack of real life experiences. Once an extensive interview has been conducted a professional will have a better idea about the child's real life experiences.

2. LIMITED ABILITY TO EXPLAIN THINGS

Children sometimes make up stories and confuse details of events because of a limited ability to explain things. Many young children have a limited vocabulary and they do not know enough words to accurately describe what has happened to them. This makes situations really confusing for social workers, psychologists, child protective specialists, and police officers who are investigating possible cases of abuse. A professional may be recording the words a child is saying without getting an accurate picture of what really occurred.

Another problem that occurs for children is that they may not understand why some things happen. They become confused about details and do not realize that some things happen on purpose while other things are accidents. I have observed children who feel that anything that happens to them is on purpose and that they are innocent in every encounter with another student. I had a little boy in my class who was in time-out often because he hit other children. He would bully, bother and irritate other class members all day, but if anyone did the slightest thing to him he would cry and make a big issue and story about the situation. There are children who are sneaky and pretend to be polite, but with closer observation one can see they are purposefully bothering other students or family members. These may be smart and very intelligent children who can lie beautifully to get other class and family members in trouble. A young child with a limited ability to explain things can not accurately describe what really happened during an altercation or quarrel.

As children were sitting on the carpet for story time one student stepped on another student's hand. The child runs to the teacher and tattles about the "mean child." Teachers have to be quick to explain that when his or her hand is stepped on by another student, it could be accidental and not intentional. Students then must be asked to be careful when walking around the room to avoid stepping on someone's hand. This is just an example of another situation where the child did not distinguish something that was intentional and on purpose from an incident that was accidental. When inquiring into children's cases and situations, keep in mind their limited ability to explain things.

3. PEER PRESSURE AND FAMILY INFLUENCE

Children sometimes make up stories to impress their peers or family members. They may agree with another student's story and concur with the crowd by giving into the peer or family pressure. For instance, each year when I taught in elementary schools I would have some bright and shiny new cars for the young children to play with when they finished their work. For several years in a row, I noticed that by the end of the year, the bright and shiny sports cars had all disappeared and I had only a few old trucks left. Eventually, I started confronting the students about taking the toys. One day, I had counted the cars and trucks that I passed out and I noticed that two of the cars were missing later. I started asking about the cars and I knew that two of the little boys had them hidden in their pockets. After a brief discussion about stealing and how it was not nice to take toys that did not belong to them, one of the students came forward to say he was sorry for taking the car. Instead of scolding him, I praised him for being honest. Shortly after that, the other boy came forward and said he was also sorry for taking the car. I wonder if the story would have turned out differently if the first little boy would not have apologized and kept his toy car. The other little boy would probably have given in to peer pressure and kept quiet with his car in his pocket to take home that night.

Family influence can have a powerful effect on the stories that children make up. It is not only the parents who influence children, but pressure to tell a story may come from siblings. I have students who were told by their parents to bring a dollar to the teacher for the field trip. Instead, the brother or sister creates a story whereby the brother buys a snack with the dollar and the sister tells the teacher she lost the money for the field trip. The teacher eventually figures out the story as the older brother shows up with a snack for the sister after lunch. When the parent picks up the younger sister, she asks the teacher if she received the field trip money. The teacher responds "no" and the parent questions the younger child until the truth emerges. Older siblings can be either a positive or negative influence on the younger siblings and the truthfulness of the stories they tell.

4. ADULTS CONFUSE CHILDREN

Most adults would hate to admit it, but sometimes they confuse children so much that the children make up stories or make comments that are untrue. Sometimes an adult will ask a child a long question that has several parts to it and a child may only hear or focus in on part of the question. The children may not understand a certain word from the question so that word confuses them and again they lose focus or go off on a tangent. A slang word may have a different meaning to an adult than it does to a child. I was asking a colleague about a slang word that I had heard in an at-risk school for several years. She tried to explain it to me, but cautioned me that many slang words had different meanings over the years and that they had become out dated. She told me there are new slang words used to describe different ideas in the community.

I mentioned to my colleague about the word "trippin" that I had heard parents use at my school. Some parents would say, "He was trippin" to refer to someone using drugs, while someone else would use the same word to describe a person who was acting crazy or had an attitude. The child's environment may influence how a child answers a question or tells a story about an experience.

If adults give children too much information, children may pick up on their cues and create or make-up a new story by what information the adult has told them. A child may not know what a word means, but if he or she hears a counselor, parent, or therapist say the word enough times, it starts to stick. The word then becomes part of the child's vocabulary and he or she starts using it to describe things even though the child really does not understand the meaning of the word. Professionals have to be cautious and careful not to give probing words or clues that could influence the child's thinking or just make the child give the answers the social worker wants to hear. It is important to keep questions and vocabulary words simple and at a level the child can understand in order to get honest answers from kids.

5. COVER UP OR DISTRACT A WRONG

I guess it is only natural for a child to make up a story of something he or she has done wrong so that he or she will not get into trouble. If children are afraid of getting into trouble by the parent or teacher, they may tell a different version of the story to each party. The parents and teacher may have to really talk with the student to get a clear version of the story and what happened. The children may be afraid of something or someone and fearful of getting in trouble or grounded for something they have done wrong. Storytelling can be devastating to adults who are asked to answer questions about an incident by a child who is lying or leaving out details and facts to avoid getting into trouble.

To cover up the wrong, the child may tell half-truths or give partial information about a situation. The children may not explain the whole story or give enough information to see the clear picture of what really happened. Adults need to be aware a child may be making up a story or simply rationalizing an incident to cover up something that he or she is feeling guilty about in his or her life. Professionals and parents must ask investigative questions to get a fuller picture of an incident and to verify the story is not being made up to cover a wrongdoing or mistake by the child.

FOUR PROBLEMS THAT ARISE
WHEN CHILDREN MAKE UP STORIES

A child usually does not have a clue that the story he or she is telling can create numerous problems for adults. The story as innocent, sweet and silly as the child may mean for it to sound may become twisted and misinterpreted causing major headaches for adults. The following four problem areas can impact the lives of adults from the story a child has made up.

1. DOUBT IS RAISED

Adults who trust each other may start doubting and second guessing each other from a story a child had told. For example, a divorced couple with joint custody of their children may start doubting each other after the children spend a weekend with one of the parents. The parent picking up the children usually asks them what they did for the weekend. A child might respond a number of ways to an open-ended question. Perhaps, dad had a beer that weekend and the child told mom, "We had beer." The mom then interprets that dad must have given the children a beer. The mother begins to doubt what the father is doing with the kids for the weekend. The same thing could happen when a parent rents a video. It may be a new release that the parent has not previewed and it contains one bedroom scene. The child may go home and tell the other parent that they watched "dirty movies" that weekend. The spouse starts to doubt the other parent and begins to wonder if he or she is showing pornographic movies to the children. The misinterpreted story or words a child says become major sources of doubt.

2. QUESTIONING BEGINS

A big problem that occurs for professionals is their integrity is questioned by stories children tell and the facts they distort. For instance, an experienced teacher with an excellent record of evaluation may have his or her whole career on the line. The teacher may be trying to separate two children who are fighting and throwing punches at each other. During the event, the child is hit and because the teacher is near when the "hit" happens, the child may go home and tell his or her parents that the teacher hit him or her. The teacher is questioned about the story and now his or her teaching credentials and professional position are on the line. These situations occur daily in the public schools and that is why many teachers carry professional liability insurance.

3. DETAILS ARE BLOWN OUT OF PROPORTION

You probably have heard the old saying, "That a little knowledge is dangerous." This saying really applies to some of the stories that children tell. A certain phrase a child learned at school may stick in the child's head even though the child missed the focus or was not listening to what the lesson really entailed. One year, I was teaching kindergarten and there was a lesson from the health curriculum on the topic of personal safety. A picture of boys and girls in bathing suits were shown and the children were told of the private parts of the body. They were told that no one should touch them on their private parts. The term "private parts" stuck in the children's heads. Although I thought the basic premise of the lesson was good, I found that some children misinterpreted the meaning of the lesson. In the weeks that followed the lesson, I was barraged with tattle tailing that he or she, "Touched me on my private parts". I observed the children closely and every time someone accidentally brushed up next to them or bumped into them, they would come complaining that they were "touched in their private parts." It was obvious that the children had blown out of proportion and misinterpreted the personal safety lesson.

4. CHAIN EFFECT

When children tell their stories to adults, they may not realize that it will turn into a chain effect where numerous people will become involved in their lives. A child tells a parent something the teacher said in class. The parent goes to the assistant principal and explains what he or she thinks happened in class. The assistant principal goes to the principal and shares his or her version of the story with the principal. The teacher is then called to the office and must defend him or herself to a story that has gone through three or four links in a chain. Each time the story was told, details were either added or deleted. The teacher who originally made a brief remark must now clarify his or her statement and justify the context of the remark. Additional time is spent examining how the child may have interpreted or misinterpreted what was said. The chain effect can happen in child related investigations where family case workers, social workers, psychologists, child protective specialists, law enforcement officers, lawyers and relatives take part in evaluating a child's story.

The following chapters give specific examples of how children's stories are misinterpreted, twisted, incorrectly communicated and misunderstood by adults.

CHAPTER TWO

LACK OF REAL LIFE EXPERIENCES

I had the cutest little boy in my pre-kindergarten class a few years ago. He enjoyed telling me things that happened to him at home. I knew that he had several recent deaths in his family. His grandmother died and a week later his grandfather also died. The little boy had made an interesting observation. He noticed that his grandmother had gone to the hospital and then she died. As he heard his family talk about death he realized that his grandfather had gone to the hospital first and then he died. My teacher's aide had been out sick for a week in the hospital. Marcus came to school to tell me that Mrs. Kyle had died. I promptly told him that Mrs. Kyle was in the hospital, but she was alive and coming back to school. His sincere observations based on his personal experiences were that people who went to the hospital would die. As Marcus gained more life experiences, he soon learned that not everyone who goes to the hospital dies. This is a perfect example of a child making up a story based on his lack of real life experiences. When Marcus sees other relatives and friends going to the hospital and coming home feeling better, he will realize that some people get well and some people die in the hospital.

A child's limited real life experiences often force him or her to make up a story or an answer to a question. I was presenting a role playing activity to a pre-kindergarten class in an at-risk school. Students went to a nearby farm on a field trip early in the year. Their earlier experiences with animals were very limited. Just before the class started, I showed them a picture of a mother cat and three kittens.

I asked the students, "What do we call baby cats?" I received responses like "baby bumblebees, little dogs, or little cats." These answers came from children who had limited exposure to pets. Finally, one student said "kittens," but the rest of the students did not seem to have a clue. The children had such limited life experiences with animals that they started guessing and making up responses to questions.

SLANG WORDS

Children have sometimes been exposed to the slang meanings of words or phrases and are limited in what they think certain words mean. A perfect example for young children is the word "bootie." I have had many students who feel that the word bootie is a dirty word only referring to a person's behind or bottom. When I showed the student's a knitted baby shoe and called it a bootie, they thought I was saying a dirty word. The students had never heard the word bootie used in any other context than part of a person's body. Confusion about the slang meaning of a word or phrase causes the child to close his or her mind to the actual meaning of the word.

Another example of this could be in how a teacher uses a word or phrase and how the student identifies with the same word or phrase. A teacher may be presenting a lesson on Mother's Day. The teacher begins by sharing with the students about the special day to honor mothers in May. The students in some at-risk schools refer to Mother's Day as the day the mother's get their government welfare checks. A person coming to question a child about an incident that happened on Mother's Day may not be aware of the meaning and details of the story the child tells. This can cause confusion for a professional because the child's understanding of a word may be strongly influenced by a cultural setting or home and community environment. A mistake can be made in accurately reporting the details of a particular incident because a child's life experiences may differ from the professional who is questioning and recording information given in the child's story.

THE CHILD'S POINT OF VIEW

Children can become unrelenting if they feel that their point of view is correct. I remember an incident where students were released from school for a Friday holiday. A student thought that since school was not held on that particular Friday school did not meet on any Friday. He went home and had his mother almost convinced that there was no school on Fridays. However, she decided to call me to verify if he needed to come to school on Fridays and I confirmed to her that there were classes every Friday. The child assumed from his limited real life experiences that because there was no school on one Friday that every Friday was an off day from school. His mother tried to explain to him that there was probably school on Friday, but he refused to listen to her. The boy became more determined and told his mother that his teacher said, "There was no school on Fridays." The mother became uncertain after listening to the child's plea that he was certain there was no school. A call to the school teacher gave the parent some reassurance, but that child was unrelenting and felt he was correct until mom made that call.

A child's limited real life experiences may cause him or her to become frustrated at even the smallest concerns or matters. I was preparing the students in my class for a field trip. I explained that each child should bring one dollar to pay for bowling on the field trip and I held up a one dollar bill for the class. A young boy told his mother about the money and the next morning she handed the little boy four quarters to pay for the field trip. The boy told his mother, "That's not right, I need a dollar." His mother tried to explain to him that four quarters was the same as a one dollar bill. The boy took the money to school and when I asked if that was the field trip money, he said, "no." The boy felt that because he did not have a one dollar bill identical to one the teacher had shown him the previous day, he did not have the appropriate money for the field trip. His lack of understanding came from his limited experience and knowledge about money. The child made up an answer or explanation because he did not understand that his mother had a dollar in quarters that was of equal value to his teacher's dollar.

I was conducting a home visit one day and a parent told me that her son repeated everything I told him in class. She told me, "You do not think he is listening, but he remembers almost everything you teach in your lessons." I wonder if parents realize that the child repeats and listens to the things they say in the same way. When a parent is getting angry on the telephone, having a fight with a spouse, or bad mouthing a neighbor, there is often some little ears that pickup what the parent is saying. What children do not realize is that some of the things being said in conversations are true, but some of the information is gossip or idle chit-chat. A child may take gossip as face value and repeat it as a true story. The child has had such limited real life experiences that he or she may not be able to distinguish actual important information about events or people from that of gossip in family and neighborhood circles.

FAMILY LIFE EXPERIENCES

Adults take for granted that children understand the family structure and its relationship to the age of people. It was so interesting to hear a child make a remark to a teacher as he arrived to school one day. The teacher was a male in his early twenties and his roommate of about the same age dropped him off for work at the school. As the teacher closed the door of the truck, several elementary students observed him. One of the students then remarked, "Is that your son?" The teacher looked astonished as he shook his head and responded, "Do I look old enough to have a son that age?" As strange as it might seem to adults, we sometimes assume children have a greater understanding of people. When I ask students who is picking them up from school, I never seem to get a straight answer. Children often identified the person with a smile to acknowledge that they knew who was picking them up that day. However, they seemed unable to describe whether that person was an aunt, uncle, cousin, brother or sister, godparent or just a family friend. Children have difficulty describing situations accurately when they lack experience to give details about family.

There are times when children make up stories because they hear their parents talk about real life experiences. The child may lack full information about real life events, but he or she may use things the parents have said, done or dreamed about as a basis for the story. A professional observing and evaluating a child's story must not overlook where the child gets the information for his or her story. I think of my childhood and how I was raised with a large family where money was real tight. Many of the family conversations were geared around the topic of money. There were always discussions on how to make extra money to pay the bills or get by until the next month. The stories I told as a child were related to my parent's life experiences. My father had dreamed for years of moving from our small dirt farm (a small acreage) to a large farm or ranch. With seven children, it was almost impossible for him to save money for his dream to come true.

The stories I made up as a child were created for me to live my father's dream. I was always telling stories to my relatives. I was going to save up a million dollars and buy my father the biggest farm in Oklahoma. I spent hours with my dad feeding the pigs each night and I told stories of how I was going to a be a pig farmer when I became an adult. When I talk to my relatives as an adult, they cannot believe how much I have changed. They comment that, "You are very quiet now, but as a child you talked for hours making up stories." I remember how my Uncle Bobby would say, "Susie, talk is cheap and dreams are free so you do all of it you want." I know my family and relatives laugh at some of the tall tales I told as a child but I really believe the stories were told to satisfy a wish that my father's dreams would come true. I did not have enough real life experience to understand the issues involved in financing a large farm, but I felt my stories satisfied future possibilities for my father's dream.

I smile as a child comes to my class and tells me, "I am going to buy a cadillac or a monster truck." I meet the child's parents and I soon understand where the child is getting his or her ideas to make up a story. Some children have had positive and wholesome real life experiences, while other children are in discouraging life situations that provide the basis of their stories. The child's bad attitude and anguish in the story could be the result of a money situation that is less than perfect. It is important to get a true picture of the child's real life experiences. A child that seems to be in positive home setting and is making up stories may be trying to express hurt or pain about something that happened to him or her. A child in a family that has financial and emotional problems on a daily basis may be melancholy or discouraged with the families' everyday struggles as he or she expresses a story. The children's real life experiences have an impact on their role in the story.

UNDERSTANDING A CHILD'S LIMITED EXPERIENCES

Sometimes a child will say something that is opposite of what he or she really means to say. A pre-kindergarten student was sitting at the table and he needed a fork. Instead of asking his teacher for a fork, the child looked at her and said, "I am eating with my hands." The teacher looked and the child was just sitting at the table looking at her. It was simply his way of relating to the teacher that he needed a fork. A child may also get opposite words confused. A little boy in class commented that he had a girlfriend. A four year old girl looked over at him and said, "You're too old to have a girlfriend". What she really meant to say was, "You are too young to have a girlfriend." The little girl knew that her comment was related to the boy's age, but she had trouble expressing it. She might have been thinking that he could have a girlfriend when he was older, but the idea of being young or old was confusing because of her lack of experiences.

Children use words to express ideas and places in their environment, even if they do not know what they mean. I asked a student in my class if he had ever eaten at McDonalds. He replied, "Yes, at the ghetto McDonalds." I asked him if he knew what the word ghetto meant and he said, "no." The child lived in the housing projects and a new McDonalds had recently been built on a nearby corner. The child had heard the word ghetto and it was part of the language he had listened to in his environment, but he did not perceive the meaning of a ghetto. His lack of real life experiences, allowed him to use slang words and expressions often, that he did not comprehend. He was picking up language experiences at home, at school, in the park, and from the neighborhood where he played outside and walked up and down the sidewalks.

Children can rehash a story over many times. A child at school might love the story of the *Three Little Pigs* and want to hear it hundreds of times. In the same way, a child may want to tell a story about a big birthday party that she is going to have on her next birthday. Each time she tells the story it is a little bit different. She might tell the story emphasizing all the friends that she is going to invite to the party. The next time she tells the story she might highlight the type of cake to eat at the party. Yet, another rendition of the story would be about all the toys she wants for her birthday. This is a child's way to visualize the story. She does not have the details of the party figured out and by repeating and retelling the story she can place herself into many roles.

An adult may not always think that a child's story is as interesting as the child thinks it is to him or her. A four year old girl told me a story that happened to her at the grocery store. She told me how her cousin corrected a little boy who put his M & M's in the wrong place on the candy bar rack. The four year old girl told me this story three times. She thought it was the most exciting story she had ever told. It was apparently a memorable day for her at the grocery store. I really do not know if she was more intrigued about the part of the story of the little boy putting his M & M's in the wrong candy rack or of the other things that happened at the store. Adults may not find everything about a child's story as unique, novel or extraordinary, but the child may have a different angle or point of view based on his or her limited life experiences.

If children have difficulty coming up with a word or answer, they will pull something out of their past life experiences. I was asking children the name of a blanket in a story that we had read. The correct answer to the question was the name Fuzzy. One child did not know the answer so she started to guess. Her first answer was, "binky" because that was what she had called her blanket when she was younger. The next answer was "tooth fairy" because she remembered putting the blanket on her bed the night that the tooth fairy came to her house. Her next reasonable guess for it was "Santa Claus" as she knew she had her favorite blanket on the bed the night that Santa stopped by her house. Each answer the young girl guessed related back to her limited life experiences. She was not thinking about the texture or fabric of the blanket, but how she had used the blanket in her life. Children can pull many different answers from their experiences.

Sometimes children will start to make a silly statement that makes sense in some situations until they discover it is not true in all cases. This occurs because children have had limited real life experiences. A five year old boy in a predominately African-American class was teasing his friends at the lunch table. He would say, "I know what color your mom is." Then after a brief pause, he would respond "same color as you are." The silly statement worked okay on the students who were the same color as their parents. However, he made the statement to a mixed race child who had a white mother and a black father. The black student responded, "My mom is not the same color as I am, she is white." The boy making the statement had his eyes opened to the fact that not all parents and children were the same color or looked alike. Children playing in a neighborhood of primarily one race or ethnic group have not had much experience seeing other races or cultures. Once they are older and their experiences broadened, they will discover many things.

A child may picture an incident in his or her head and so every story he or she tells may have that incident in it. I have noticed this in children as I have observed them in the classroom. One day a child told me about this wonderful party his family was going to have for his father's birthday. I assumed that his father was having an upcoming birthday and the boy had heard his family discussing the details of the party. Each day the boy would make the details of the party more exciting. One day he would share with the class how he was going to have a big barbecue at the park for the party. Another day he would talk about the beautiful cake they would eat at the party. It was not long before he invited all his friends in class to the party. The child made up stories for weeks about this party. I approached his father one day and asked if he was planning a big birthday party. The father told me, "no" and that he had no inkling how the boy had come with the idea for the party. Every story the boy shared in class was about this party for approximately four weeks. He was having a fantasy and enjoyed this story.

Children have had very limited life experiences related to people's occupations. They are still trying to figure out what the world of work is all about in life. Students will ask their teachers if they sleep and live in the school. One student even asked me when I was going to leave the school and go get a job. They have a hard time visualizing their teachers at work because school is so much fun. Children also have trouble comprehending that people are paid to perform certain jobs. During a career week at school a young woman came to read the students a story. She told the class how she worked in a hospital and that she was an office worker. It took several minutes to convince the students that other people work in the hospitals besides doctors and nurses. The students did not comprehend it until the office worker told them some of her job duties. Once she explained she used a computer and filed papers for her employer the children better comprehended her job position. The students keep asking the woman if she paid the hospital to work there. Several students kept making this statement. It took some convincing before the students understood that the hospital paid the person to work in that setting.

Young children are sometimes afraid because they do not know if some occupations are respectable or not. When a young preschool girl sees a doctor giving her brother a shot, she may think the doctor is mean because he or she made her brother cry. An ambulance driver taking away a grandparent that later dies may not seem very admirable in a child's eyes. As I mentioned earlier in the book, police officers who take parents away are seldom looked upon favorably by children. I worked in one community where child protective workers took children out of the home on a sidewalk near a school. As you can imagine, the other children in the community were horrified of social workers and child protective workers because they viewed them as tearing families apart. As children gain life experiences and grow older, they will better understand occupations.

CHAPTER THREE

LIMITED ABILITY TO EXPLAIN THINGS

WHAT DO WORDS MEAN TO CHILDREN?

Children's limited ability to explain things and describe situations is one of the major causes of confusion for adults interpreting children's stories. An adult may hear a child tell a story and take it for face value that it is true. The words that have bothered me the most over the years are he or she, "Hit me." For years as a school teacher, children would tattle he or she, "hit me." On closer observations I have found that young children use the word hit to describe many different things. A boy touches another child on the shoulder and the child tattles, "He hit me." A girl at the water fountain splashed water on the other student and the student tattles, "She hit me." Students lined up for recess accidentally bumped into each other going down the hall. They are not watching in front of them and the teacher hears the familiar, "They hit me," excuse one more time that day.

It is not only teachers and professionals who have to deal with the child's limited vocabulary and ability to explained a situation, but also the parents. A parent may have to answer and explain a situation that a child miscommunicated to a teacher, nurse or administrator. For example, a child is playing at home and she runs into mom's hand and scratches her face on her mother's wedding ring. The child comes to school on Monday morning with scratches on her face. The teacher asks the child what happened to her face and the child responds, "My mom hit me." School officials report the incident to child protective services and an investigator shows up at the parent's door to question the parent about the incident. Parents can become furious at school officials for reporting an incident. The parent is angry and distraught with child protective services for making an accusation about her character and having to defend herself in an incident that was miscommunicated by her child. As you can see from this example information was miscommunicated by the child who did not have the ability or vocabulary to adequately explain the situation to others.

I want to caution professionals writing reports and conducting investigations to be careful when a child uses the word "hit" to describe an incident. The child may not be accurately describing what happened to him or her. These children become confused about whether the incident happened on purpose or was just an accident. An example of this happened one day on the playground as I was on duty and several classes were enjoying playing in the sunshine before lunch. Suddenly, the fire alarm went off and the children were rushing to line up with their teachers. During the excitement, two children ran into each other and bumped their heads. Both children started crying and one child yelled, "He hit me." I quickly interjected that it was just an accident and that we must slow down and be careful on the playground. You can see where a child may go home and say to his or her parents that someone at school, "hit me." Be cautious because children often do not have the vocabulary and ability to explain things and describe situations that have occurred at school and in the home.

As a teacher I have had to rephrase and explain to children various situations, so they can understand them better. One day I held my hand out to explain something (You know how teachers often talk with their hands) and a student bumped into my fingernails. Her first response was, "You scratched me." I quickly corrected her, and I explained to her that I did not scratch her. She had bumped into my fingers and it was an accident. There are situations where teachers and other professionals become entangled in circumstances where they are questioned about a child's limited ability to explain a situation.

One day I was about to take a little girl's hand so we could walk down the hall because she was the line leader that day. As I reached for her hand, she responded, "Do not pull my arm." I responded, "I did not pull your arm, but I was taking your hand so we could lead the class down the hall." She was fine with that explanation and she preceded down the hall happily holding my hand. I have found that as a teacher I have to address these situations quickly because a child may add details to the story and get other students to believe and support their story. I must also be empathetic that some children may not want to hold my hand because of a bad home experience or a previous abuse situation.

Professionals need to be cautious when asking children to explain incidents related to numbers, amounts and age. If a professional asked a child what age someone was the child could answer with a broad range of responses. I used to ask my students what age or how old they thought I was. I would get responses like seven years old to one hundred years old. In the same way, if a child describes someone as big, he or she might be referring to an adult or to a small child that is a fraction taller than that child. Children have trouble explaining the difference between old and young, slow and fast, small and large, big and little, pushing and pulling, hot and cold, and other words adults take for granted.

I love to hear students talk about money in their piggy banks and money that their parents give them. One student will say, "My mother gave me a dollar," and another student will say, "My mother is going to give me one hundred thousand dollars." I have had some of the poorest students in my class tell me they are rich if they have a penny in their pockets. On the other hand, I have heard children from very wealthy families tell me stories about how broke they are and have no money. Young children have limited abilities to explain what they mean by amounts of money, numbers, ages of people and terms to describe their ideas. It is important to collect as much information as possible from a child so one can understand fully what children are communicating about their stories and accounts.

Some children make up stories or answers to questions because they do not want to appear inarticulate or simple minded. These children do not want their friends at school to call them "dumb" or "stupid." Instead of admitting that they simply do not know the answer, these children will say anything just to answer a question. I asked a young boy in the class to tell me the name of the school his sister attended. He did not know, but he would never admit that to me. The little boy told me the name of the school his sister attended was "teenagers." Perhaps his sister attended a junior high or middle school and that was the best term he could come up with to name the school. He rode by the school each day as his parents dropped off his sister and watched a group of teenagers standing at the school. The boy chose a name for the school from his experiences with that school.

Children's stories evolve from a limited ability to explain their possessions and territory. A common phrase I hear among elementary children is "That's mine." I have heard this phrase used in many different contexts. A child may say "That's mine" as he is taking (or stealing) another child's toy car. This child uses the term "That's mine" to take control of things he wants that others possess. I have also observed students using the term "That's mine" regarding the trading of their possessions. A group of children is coloring pictures together as they sit at a classroom table. A girl looks at the crayon box of the little boy next to her and says, "That's mine" as she touches his orange crayon. The orange crayons in each child's box are almost identical, but the children trade with each other. In addition, I have heard students use the statement, "That's mine" to describe things that are not theirs. A friend of the family comes driving to school and the child says, "That's mine" to refer to the friend's cars. A child might use the same phrase of, "That's mine" to refer to an airplane that just flew over the playground.

Sometimes a child may get a particular phrase in his or her head and the child uses it as part of his or her vocabulary to describe many different things in life. For example, a police officer may ask child which house she lives in and she points to a house and says, "That's mine." After an investigation, the police officer discovers the child does not live there. She may have just visited the house once before or it could be a relative's or friend's house. The young girl becomes confused because the house has similar features or is the same color as her house. The child may have had earnest intentions and much sincerity, but lacked the ability to explain in more detail about the house she where she lived.

Children may also lack the ability to properly ask for or borrow possessions from their friends so they may threaten or make harsh demands to get their way. I have noticed children about the age of four saying the phrase, "You are not my friend." They use this phrase if another child will not give them a toy. I have even observed a student using this phrase if other students look at him with a frown of disapproval. Sometimes a child will say, "You are not my friend unless you buy me something." A teacher friend shared a story about how one boy was making a harsh threat on another very impoverished student to buy him a bag of potato chips at the student store. The teacher had to explain to the student making the harsh demand that the impoverished student could not buy him any chips even if he wanted to, because he did not have any money. The student making the threat was also dealing with a power issue where he wanted to control other students at school. Issues such as control, power, attention and conflict may be part of the child's inability to explain things.

EXPRESSING FEELINGS

Children's stories can change from day to day by how children feel or what interests them in a particular day. A child draws a picture and the teacher asks the child to tell him or her about the picture. One day the child may say the picture, "is a dog" and the next day the child may tell the teacher that it is "an airplane." This is coming from a young child who is exploring and inventing the world around him or her. Every day, children develop new interests and add information to their characters. As family situations change, the stories of children change. A new baby in the family, a divorce of parents or a separation from a significant person can totally change the way a child interprets the environment around him or her. As a result, children's stories are not always consistent. A person interviewing a child only one time may not spot inconsistencies in a child's story. People dealing with children on a daily basis, such as teachers and caretakers, can observe children for long periods of time and are very aware of inconsistencies in their stories.

A child may make up a story just to express a dislike of something. A boy was riding home on the bus one day and the bus driver was treating them to pickles as a reward for good behavior. The boy disliked pickles and instead of saying, "No, thank you" or "I do not care for pickles" he made up a response. He told the bus driver that pickles make him sick. It was just an excuse so that he would not have to eat the pickles. Some children will quickly learn excuses not to eat those, "delicious" (just kidding) school lunches. They will tell their teachers that they have allergies to a food they do not like. The teacher checked with the parents and the children often do not have an allergy, but the children liked to use this excuse to express a dislike of something. Some students have medical concerns and food allergies, but there are also students who use the allergy stories as an expression or excuse not to eat their food. Students also pick up on the excuse, "I have already eaten at home." If they can avoid even tasting the school lunch, they will use all avenues to avoid eating the school food that they dislike so much. Parents respond to stories that children tell about food very seriously. Teachers, school food service workers and administrators often have to clarify children's stories that are based on the child's dislike of a particular food.

POOR LISTENING SKILLS

A child's limited ability to explain things may be a result of poor listening skills or a short attention span. When a teacher presents a lesson or a guest speaker tells a story to children, it is hard to tell which details of the lesson or story will stick in a particular child's mind. A guest speaker presented a self-concept lesson with puppets. One of the puppets was a puppy who was recovering from drug and alcohol problems. The young students had a problem understanding the lesson. They related a puppy as being wholesome and good, while drugs and alcohol were bad in the children's eyes. Some of the children became upset this cute little puppy supposedly had drug and alcohol problems. The story of the puppets may make perfect sense to an older elementary student, but for a very young child to understand and explain the intent or purpose of the story may be difficult. If a story is long, drawn out and confusing, the young child may only be absorbing and ingesting small bits and pieces of the story. As a result, some children do not get the main idea of the story and lose the meaning of the story. A child retelling the puppet story may have a totally new version of the story.

Poor listening skills may also hinder a child's ability to explain situations or tell of events in a story. I read a small group of pre-kindergarten children a cute story one day about a mouse and his favorite blanket. I used props and tried to make the story interesting for the students. They seemed interested in the story because they laughed at some parts and their facial expressions showed excitement about the story. I had prepared a list of five very simple questions about the story and I thought the students would be able to answer them without any trouble. I was wrong because the students could not even tell me the name of the mouse in the story. The mouse's name was read twenty times in the short story, but the students did not remember. A colleague of mine suggested that students really need help in learning to focus in and visualize a story. She told me that she often has the students lie on the floor with their eyes closed. The students can listen to the story by becoming more focused on what the teacher is telling in the story. They can also visualize the development of the story and the characters. My colleague would have the students sit up at the end of the story and then ask questions to them. She felt this technique was helpful in improving their listening skills.

A child with poor listening skills may be very inattentive to details and pertinent information. Children may miscommunicate information that parents or teachers give them because they have not listened for correct directions or accurate details. A social worker or police officer may not get a reliable and trustworthy story from this type of child. The child may be very sincere, but errors, mistakes, and misinformation could be part of the child's poor listening habits.

CONFUSING INFORMATION

There are children who have a hard time dealing with questions from adults regarding people's names. The child may be telling a story using a variety of nicknames. There are children who only know how to identify themselves by their nicknames. These children really do not know what their names are and often the parents have not taken time to teach the children their real names. I was teaching in an at-risk school and each year as I called the roll I would say a child's name and get no response. I would say the name several more times just in case the children were not paying attention or listening as I called the roll. I knew the particular child was in my class because I would put a name tag on the child when he or she arrived with his or her parent. I would then ask the child what his or her name was and I would usually get the nickname. These children only knew their identity by the nickname they had in their families. Children's limited ability to identify themselves by their real names makes it difficult for social workers, teachers, child protective specialists and law enforcement officials who are trying to collect accurate information on the child.

Children in my class would often tattle the very familiar phrase "He or she said a cuss word." Early in my teaching career, I would go to the child I suspected of saying the cuss word and tell him or her to talk nicely at school. Several years later in my teaching career, I started to question the child who was tattling. I would ask the child what word the other student had said. I started to get some very interesting answers. For example, a child would say the word "dirt" and another child would say it was a cuss word. I soon observed that some children think almost every word is a cuss word. They have trouble distinguishing bad words from everyday vocabulary. For some children to run and tattle to the teacher is a way to get attention. The cuss word tattling can just become an excuse for the child to run to the teacher for a moment of that prized attention.

Children hear words on television and they start to use them even if the meaning is unclear to them. I have heard young elementary students come to class and use words like "let's hump" or "sex." They even misunderstand the words they use in their language. One child kept using the word "pregnant," but it was evident the child did not know what the word meant. The child kept pointing to his tooth and saying the tooth was pregnant. The child meant to say it was his permanent tooth that hurt. He was totally unaware that he was using an incorrect word to describe his tooth until adults started to correct him. Another child kept telling me that her father was pregnant and that he was going to have a baby. Although dad had a very big stomach the child had not learned that only women give birth to babies. She thought dads had baby boys and moms had baby girls. Children become confused because they are learning so many new things when they are young that they have not processed all the new information and made sense of it all.

Children can have limited ability to explain an injury or illness. A professional observing a child should not become too concerned if the child is crying. Some children can put out the loudest, bellowing cry over the smallest bump or scratch. I have had students cry very loudly and show me a tiny scratch that I could barely see. Often, I would tell a child to run some water on his or her finger and the crying would quickly stop. Children get their needs confused with an illness. I have noticed that children complain about their stomachs in the mid-morning of school. A child will say, "I have a stomachache," when he or she really meant to say, "I am hungry." I have observed this behavior many times nearly thirty minutes before lunch. Sometimes a hug from the teacher and a little reassurance that lunch is on the way will make the stomach ache disappear. A small hurt or pain can be over exaggerated in a child's cry and inability to explain even a slight medical condition or a minor injury.

When a child has limited ability to explain situations he or she may get totally confused about the details of a story. One of my students lived in an at-risk community and there was a shooting outside his home. He overheard family members discussing the incident and he knew that someone was killed. There was also an ambulance in front of his house that he had viewed from his front window. He knew that someone was killed and that here was an ambulance outside of his house. The child was telling the story to his classmates at school, but he was not able to explain what had happened in his front yard. The child told the students, "An ambulance killed the man and took off." The child could not explain how the individual was killed, but he did make the connection the ambulance driver killed the man. The child did not understand the purpose of the ambulance in this incident. The young boy knew that something terrible had happened in his front yard, but he could not explain it. Children are often sheltered from the truth or the harsh details of a story. They are trying to put the details of the story together with limited information.

CHAPTER FOUR

PEER PRESSURE AND FAMILY INFLUENCE

One of the first things a public school teacher learns is not to believe everything the students tell them. Unfortunately, some parents and professionals have become very gullible to believing some of these stories from children. Many times I have observed students whose stories are far-fetched and told to other students to make friends or be in with a group of buddies. I have seen students make a comment like, "My dad drinks beer." Before long, the whole class is telling how their dad's drink beer (even if they do not know their dad). The point is that the child is simply telling the story to be part of the class discussion with their peers.

In an at-risk school where I taught, one student would mention that, "My mom's in jail." Again, a number of students would start talking about the time their mom was in jail. I clarified the details of the story to the students that not everyone's mother was in jail and that some of their mothers brought them to school. If children feel they get attention or approval from their peers, they will be a part of a story even if they know it is not true.

One of the first things that I noticed young children around the age of four years old start saying to each other is either, "You are my friend," or "You are not my friend." Naturally, to make friends, children will agree with the other person's story and that is a wonderful example of peer pressure.

Young children also notice the attention they get from their peers when they tell an interesting and imaginative story. I have watched students eating lunch together at small tables. One child tells a story about a cartoon character or a scary movie about "Chucky." Suddenly, the other students are telling a made up story about this television or movie character. To be part of the conversation at the lunch table, children are joining in the story telling process. As innocent and creative for students as this may seem, it only takes one upset parent over an incident and suddenly the teacher has to answer for a student's behavior.

Children also make up stories because of family influence. Their parents may tell them to lie or they may just simply observe their parents telling lies and stories so they start to tell them at school. Some young children are so honest they can not agree with these stories. I had a student who was absent from school for several days. When I asked her where she had been, her first response was, "My mom told me I was not supposed to tell you." Of course, later that day, it slipped out in another discussion that mom had been in California. Children become confused by what family members say and they have trouble keeping stories straight, so the details become mixed up and the facts become blurred. This is why professionals have to be careful in believing children's stories. There are so many influences in children's lives and they are not all good. Children sometimes have doubts, insecurities, and extreme pressure from peers and family members to tell a story a certain way.

MAKING DREAMS COME ALIVE

A few children make up stories because they want their dreams to come true. A young boy whose parents divorce will often make up stories in an attempt to bring the parent back into his life. He would tell stories about how his father took him on a fishing trip that was neat or how they went to McDonalds together. In reality, the boy's father had not been to see him in months. The boy wanted his father to be in his life so much that he imagined and made up stores to discover the father that was not in his life. The child may also be making up a story to impress his friends when he hears them talking about their fathers. Not to be outdone by his friends' neat stories about how their fathers take them to baseball practice, he creates a story about his absent father to match his friends' stories.

I have noticed that young children may have different versions of their stories in divorce cases where children are trying desperately to please both parents. Some children even feel as if the divorce is their fault so they will say anything to please each parent. The version of the child's story sounds twisted and confused because the child is being influenced by two powerful forces in his or her life, the parents. Just the simple act of picking up a child after school becomes a source of concern for the child. I hear elaborate stories by children about how mom or dad is going to pick them up from school and take them to the movies, out to eat, and to the park. Often the other parent, who picks the child up everyday shows up as usual even though the child has a wonderful picture in his or her mind of how the day would end. Most young children love their parents so it is understandable that they are trying very hard to gain affection and attention from parents even it means changing their stories. Professionals must not forget this important side in evaluating the truthfulness of children's stories and reality.

There are occasions when a child's story starts out true, but becomes exaggerated or overstated by family or peer influences. Carl came to school one Monday morning to share how his house was robbed the previous weekend. He started telling his friends the story during the breakfast. The other boys at his table began asking questions and showing a great interest in his story. Once Carl knew he had the attention of his peers, he started to add details to his story. Suddenly, he was telling his friends that he, "Tore off the gang banger's head," and that he killed the person who broke into his house. What started out as a simple explanation that Carl's house was robbed, turned into a huge tale of suspense, intrigue, and excitement. My observations were that Carl's story started out true, but turned into fantasy when he noticed that he was the focal point of attention from his classmates. This was positive attention from his peers, whom he often had disputes and disagreements. Carl savored this moment of wonderful attention from the other children in the class and he took full advantage of exaggerating and making up parts of the story.

Children may also misinterpret their parents threats or claims. Some children, in particular those raised in at-risk situations, hear their parents making threats, accusations, or exaggerated claims against other people. The child may not understand that this is just talk and it is the way that some parents deal with anger and disappointment. The parent may threaten to harm another person as a defense mechanism to protect his or her feelings. The child observing the parent's behavior may take what the parent has said as a true and literal message. The child came to school and told everyone his father was going to beat the crap out of the next door neighbor and get rid of the neighbor. Professionals examining stories such as these must see if the circumstances are for real or if the child is overstating, misjudging or misrepresenting statements of exaggerated claims by their parents as true events.

I have also observed that some students tell wonderful and fascinating stories to their peers. The story begins with normal everyday occurrences and then develops into a full blown monster story. The child tells the class that as she is sleeping in her bed a monster appears. She grabs the flashlight and looks at the strange monster and then cries for her mother. After the child has fully gained the attention of their classmates and teacher, she happens to throw in at the end of the story that it was all a dream. I have had numerous students use "the dream" to justify their stores to their classmates. When a class of students is sitting at a cafeteria table for lunch "the dream" stories run rapid among the students. One student shared details about the strange and wonderful things that happened in his or her dream. Suddenly there is a domino effect of other students making their stories better than the last story. The anxious students start interrupting and talking over each other just to interject more exciting details of the made up story.

Professionals analyzing the student's stories must not overlook that it could be a dream.

A child's tale of adventure is influenced by family member's discussions of television programs. My parents spent many hours watching television during cold winter months. I was growing up in Oklahoma during the oil boom. There were many news programs on television of people going up to Alaska to work on the pipe line. I listened attentively to my father as he would talk about pulling up this stakes and moving the family to Alaska. After a while, I really began to believe that my family was going to move to Alaska. I remember going to school in the fifth grade and telling my teacher that we were going to move to Alaska. Our class had just seen a movie about people living in Alaska and that reaffirmed my belief that my family was going to move thousands of miles away from Oklahoma. As I grew older, I realized that my parents had no intention of ever moving out of the state of Oklahoma.

My family was such a strong influence on me as a young child that I sometimes took everything they told me as fact or truth. If my parents said something, then I really believed it to be true and honest. I did not understand the process of discussion that my parents were experiencing as part of their everyday lives. My youthful perspective did not allow me to see that my parents could be only pondering about these things. I was not able to allow them to make speculations or explore options and ventures in their lives. While my parents were deliberating, contemplating, meditating, or just joking about things in life, I was taking the information to be literal and serious. The story I made up about moving to Alaska was very sincere and heartfelt, but the story was untrue because I did not understand my parent's nature to contemplate life's issues. It is not uncommon for children to take a speculative statement made by parents or another adult and turn it into a believable and true sounding story.

CHILDREN'S CAMARADERIE

The made up story of a child can be related to the child's camaraderie with siblings, relatives or friends. The minister at the church I attended shared a story with the congregation. He said that as his oldest son was scolded for something, his youngest son threw a temper tantrum. The younger child could not orally express it, but his actions were clear that he was furious that his brother was in trouble with mom. Children at school do this as well. For example, a little girl started crying when she was sent to time out. Another little girl goes up and puts her arm the crying girl. She consoles her by saying, "It's all right, the teacher was mean to you and I will be your friend." This is a good example of how a child's story is overshadowed by emotion, hurt feelings, and supportive friends to ease the pain. It is not a good indication of what the child was really in trouble for at school, but how the camaraderie of friends can change the emphasis of the story.

Some stories result from a child's image that being bad is a good thing. For many years, students used the phrases, "He is bad, or that's bad" to say someone was good or that they liked something. Being bad became a way of getting attention from peers. Children watch television programs and movies that sometimes depict the "bad" people as good, tough and popular. A teacher colleague of mine was teaching a lesson on police officers. She role-played a skit with her students and many of them wanted to be the "bad" person in the skit. Instead of wanting to role-play the police officer that represented someone helpful in our society, the students wanted to be the bad person who stole the woman's person. One child even commented that he, "enjoyed and liked being bad." Children sometimes see an example in a play or on television and they want to become that bully or bad person. Follow-up activities help clarify rewards of positive behavior and consequences of bad behavior.

It is not unusual for children to use words that they do not understand the meaning. A child may have heard another student or relative use the word so he or she may start using it even if the meaning is unclear. There was a perfect example in my classroom as I was teaching a lesson on safety. I had just shared with the students that they should not talk to strangers. A little girl from a rough neighborhood raised her hand and shared a story about how a young girl in the community was pulled into a car and raped. She had shared a serious and sincere story with the class. A little boy in the class was not listening closely and only heard one word in her story. The word that stuck in his head was "rape." He then told me that he and his brother were "raped by a monster." It was clear the child did not know the meaning of the word "rape," but it was a word he liked to use. When evaluating a child's story, the observer must listen closely to see if the child may be pulling information from the wind and other children.

GETTING THEIR WAY

As my sister, who is the mother of seven children tells me, "Kids make up stories just to get their way." If you think about it, children are egocentric and they think the world revolves around them. Their stories are often about themselves. They like to tell stories about going somewhere fun, or buying something expensive, or learning to do something difficult. Many of these stores are made up to build the child's self-image to peers or family members. In large families, children fight for attention, so stories become competitive in getting affection from the parents. Children may turn on each other and camaraderie disappears as children try to get their way. My sister told me a childhood story that I had totally forgotten. We had both sold raffle tickets for a school fundraising event. Apparently, we combined out tickets so that we could win the grand prize. The teachers announced my name as I won the photo album. My sister remembers clearly that I told her, "I sold the tickets and the photo album is all mine." It was my story to keep the photo album to myself and get my way.

Children wanting to get their way may use persuasive techniques and even incorporate threats to adults and peers. After a child has begged and pleaded for something, he or she may use extreme measures to aggressively get his or her way. The children may threaten to run away if their parents do not let them go to the movies. Children can give different versions of the story to mom and dad and try to get at least one parent on their side when their request gets to the final bargaining at the kitchen table. Children may pull their parents aside and present requests in private instead of the full view of the other siblings. Some children will even go to greater extremes and threaten to, "kill themselves," if they do not get to do what they want. Be aware that some children want to be in control and have total power and authority in situations. These children feel that by threatening a parent or making an adult feel sorry for them that they will get their way.

STRONG PARENTAL INFLUENCE

Parental influence is extremely strong in shaping the ideas and stories that children tell each other. I was in a hardware store one day and overheard two young boys talking. It was a small community in Texas so I could feel the bias and prejudices pour out of their conversation. They were discussing whether people drove American-made cars or foreign made cars. In their eyes, if people did not drive a certain kind of car or truck, they were worthless. The determination and strong-willed nature of the boys as they discussed the various types of vehicles was amazing. It was very obvious that their beliefs and opinions about cars and the people who drive them were based on the convictions, judgments, and suspicions of their parents. As children become older, they will gain more skills to sort information, separate fact and opinion, and make informed decisions. A young child who has not developed a fair-minded and impartial attitude will tell a story from the parent's perspective and not realize the bias judgments and extreme views as part of the story.

Sometimes parents make a big issue if a child says, "I hurt my back or my arm." A child's statement may be taken out of proportion and teachers or day care workers must defend themselves to angry parents. There was a young boy in my class who never mentioned to my teacher's aide or me that he had hurt himself. He went home from school and convinced his mother he hurt his back at school after being pushed into a bookshelf. I really believe that this incident never occurred, but the child received so much attention from his parents that he kept the story going for weeks. The mother told me of the boy's constant complaining of his back and that she was going to take him to the doctor. The doctor conducted a full examination and x-rays on the boy's back and determined there was nothing wrong with the boy's back. The parent was not convinced that the child was making up the story until he had a full medical examination.

After years of teaching in the public schools, I observed closely when a child comes complaining about an injury. I will ask the child to sit down for a few minutes if I believe the injury is not serious. Usually, the child will desire to go back and play on the playground a few minutes later. I ask the child a very important question before I let him or her play. I simply say, "Do you feel okay?" The child usually responds, "yes." If parents question me about an incident, I tell them the child sat for a few minutes and when I asked if he or she was feeling okay, the child responded, "yes." This allows me as a professional to know that I addressed the student about the situation. It is helpful if another teacher or co-worker observes me asking the child this question, because I then have a witness that sees the child going back to play. It is amazing how quick a child forgets a hurt arm when he or she wants to play with a sand toy or go down the slide.

Parental influence is so strong in the lives of children that it has an impact on how children behave and the things they say and do. I have observed children in role-playing activities during free play in the dramatic play center. Young children who are four to five years old will pretend to smoke cigarettes and make up stories about getting drunk or shooting someone. Many of these stories have themes introduced by family members and others in the surrounding community of the child's home. Parents may not even realize the impact that television has on the child's stories and behavior. Parents who do not closely monitor the television watching may not realize the information the child is receiving from television. As a teacher, I would often discuss with parents that the child was bringing bad language to school. Many parents just could not realize where the child was coming up with inappropriate words or describing detailed sexual acts. Children who are unsupervised by adults may be watching large amounts of violence, sex and negative behaviors that are influencing the things they say and stories they tell to others.

Parents have many opportunities to help encourage positive and constructive behaviors in their children. Educators, social workers, and law enforcement officers must not pass up the chance to inspire parents to talk with their children and reinforce positive and well-grounded behavior. Older siblings may be watching programs that are unsuitable for very young children. Children become confused by the violence and the reality of television with the real world. A child may be planning something that is self-destructive because he or she distorts an exaggerated claim on a television program. Peer pressure and family influences can affect the stories and details a child tells to the world. On the other hand, peers and family can also help children question and rethink the information in a story.

CHAPTER FIVE

ADULTS CONFUSE CHILDREN

I remember observing my students in class one day and how confused they were as the school counselor made a presentation about drugs. She asked what she thought was a simple question to young children. The students raised their hands eager to answer, but their comments allowed me to see they were confused by the questions the counselor had asked them. The question she asked the students was, "Does anyone in your family smoke grass?" Every one of the students (about 30 children) raised their hands and shouted, "yes." Some of the students only heard the smoking part of the question and they kept making comments like, "My dad smokes cigarettes or my aunt smokes." One or two of the street smart kids probably knew what she was really talking about, but the other students did not have a clue. The cutest comments were, "We have grass in our yard," and "My dad cuts the grass with a lawnmower." Some children were probably visualizing the big yard of green grass on the playground as the counselor was trying to present a lesson about drug use. The students were confusing their experiences about grass, with an adult's bewildered remark about grass as a drug. The adult in this case did not even clarify what the meaning of the word grass was and she assumed the students all understood what it meant. Her lesson was over their heads, so they started making confusing remarks. Adults must consider the age of the children they are speaking to and how they translate these words into pictures.

RELIGIOUS EXPERIENCE CONFUSION

On occasion, a child will come to school and share confusing stories related to religious experiences. The child may get God mixed up with something he or she is studying in school. In December, the class studied about Santa Claus and a student asked, "Does God live on the North Pole?" Sometimes a child will talk about God to describe good behavior and the devil to describe bad behavior. The child starts misbehaving in class and another student may point out to the misbehaving student that he or she is acting like a devil. When one's family member dies, it is not uncommon for children to talk about going to heaven. Sometimes a child may apply something out of the Bible to a real life situation. A teacher once told me that a student kept telling him that his father lay in a morgue for three days and arose from the dead. When the teacher talked to the parent he found out the father was a minister in a charismatic church and that the student had misinterpreted Jesus' burial and resurrection as that of his father.

The whole idea about a "God" is confusing for most children. When children hear adults talk about "God," they may only pick up bits and pieces of what the adults are saying. One four year old boy told me, "God was his father." Another little girl commented, "I have a godmother and she is a god, too." Children hear adults comment about God and spiritual things and they are exploring and trying to put the picture together. Children may try to bring God down to a level they can understand. Therefore, a child will relate God to the world that he or she knows best. A child may make God a guest at her tea party as she serves tea to her dolls or plans a birthday party. Some children may blame the bad things that happen to them on God or the devil. The innocence of these stories is apparent in most cases because the child is learning and processing a number of spiritual ideas.

It is not uncommon for children to become confused by something they hear or observe in church services. As a child, I attended a slumber party with about five other little girls. The family hosting the slumber party took us to a Wednesday church service. It was a powerful and emotional service on sin. The older sister of the girl hosting the slumber party became very emotional and started crying. The minister asked the people in the congregation to come forward and confess their sins. When the older sister decided to go forward with her heartfelt confession, you will never guess who followed her up to the front of the church. Each of the little girls followed the older sister to the front of the church, and the preacher asked us if we wanted forgiveness for our sins. We did not have a clue what was going on that night and when I went home and told my mother that story the next day she was furious. I understand now, my mother's rage as she wrote a note to the mother of the student who had the slumber party. As young children, we did not understand the complexity of the preacher's sermon that Wednesday night. We were in a new setting and he wanted to do the right thing and follow directions. The older sister's emotional experience and the preacher waving his hands for us to come forward was enough to totally confuse us. It was confusing, because in my own church I had gone forward many times for children's worship or to hear a bible story geared toward a children's message. The experience I had at that Wednesday church service has haunted me for years. It bothered me to think that as a young, innocent child an adult's strong emotional message would leave little girls very confused.

QUESTIONS AND ANSWERS

Sometimes adults confuse children by asking questions that automatically elicit a yes or no response without getting a true picture of what the child is thinking. For instance, an adult wants to find out if the child enjoyed his or her Christmas presents and asks, "Did you see Santa Claus?" The child immediately answers, "no." Later, the adult hears the child talking about the presents he or she received for Christmas. The adult could have asked about what toys the child received over

Christmas and found a more satisfactory answer. The child may have known that Santa or someone left the presents, but because he or she did not see Santa Claus that Christmas night, the honest response was no. The yes or no question solicited a respond, but it did not give enough information about the type of Christmas the child really experienced. Professionals collecting and recording information on children must ask more than a few yes or no questions to investigate, search and inquire into the child's true mind and feelings. In addition, if children are not paying adequate attention to the questions asked by professionals they may tend to answer yes or no without thinking. There are also children who answer yes to questions without paying attention to the way the investigator phrased the question. Some children are afraid to say no because they think they might get in trouble for saying the wrong answer. The professional investigating the child's statements should set the goal of getting an honest and clear picture of the situation. He or she must be aware that the child may not give enough information to provide a clear picture if questions are phrased for a yes or no answer.

Adults sometimes give very vague directions to children and so the child does not think he or she has done anything wrong. The child tries to explain the situation, but has a different perspective of the adult. I was observing some young children during a library storytime. A teacher's aide kept correcting a child and the child was ignoring her. The child was sitting on his knees when he should have been on his bottom so the other students sitting behind him could see the book. The teacher's aide commented, "Mike, sit down," and the child ignored her. She commented again, "Mike, sit down," and again the child ignored her. In a stern voice the woman said, "Mike, sit down, now". The child looked at her in a calm voice and said, "I am sitting." The teacher's aide should have given Mike more specific directions that she wanted him to sit on his bottom. Mike's perspective of the situation was totally different from that of the teacher's aide. When Mike has to explain to his mother what happened during the library storytime, his story will be different from the one the teacher's aide tells the parent. Mike became confused by the vague directions given to him by an adult, so his explanation of the situation was that he was sitting and following directions. If the adult wanted Mike to do more than that, she would have to give more specific directions so that Mike knew what she wanted him to do.

Children's stories sometimes are a result of the experiences of adults playing tricks on them or confusing them. For instance, a mother has some sugar cereal for her son, but he is only allowed to eat it on special occasions. She does not store it with the other cereal, but hides it on top of the refrigerator. Her young son spots the bag of cereal on the edge of the refrigerator and has found the hiding place. He looks up at the cereal and makes up a story of how he is going to fly up to the top of the refrigerator and get the cereal. The child knew he was not big enough to climb and get the cereal or tall enough to stand on a chair to reach it. However, in this story he has found a way to imagine reaching the forbidden cereal.

Adults sometimes confuse children by not giving them straight answers to their questions. I remember asking my parents for things as a child and their standard answers were, "We will see." I loved horses as a child and there were many beautiful quarter horses I so desired. I would beg my mother for a bigger horse and she would say, "We will see." I would then go to school and tell my friends of this wonderful quarter horse that I was going to buy when my parents saved up the money for it. Later in life, I learned that, "We will see," was just a polite way of saying, "no." However, as a child, I thought, "We will see" meant there was a strong possibility that I could get that horse. Therefore, my stories evolved from the information adults gave me. The adult was my parent whom I trusted and believed in so much. I sincerely thought that my mother would help me get that horse as I told the stories to my friends.

Adults say other things to children when they ask for things. Sometimes a parent will tell a child a straight answer to a question such as yes or no. Later, the parent changes his or her mind or tries to distract the child from the original request. There are occasions when a parent or adult will tell a child, "another time." This phrase might be appropriate at the supermarket when the child is begging for a candy bar. The child is not allowed a candy bar on that particular day, because it will ruin his or her supper. The parent is leaving open the possibility that the child may have a candy bar on another occasion. A child hears his or her parents say phrases like: "Later, another day; We will see in the future; or, Go ask your grandparents." The child also observes the actions, behavior and honesty the parents use in giving them a full picture of reality. Simple responses adults give to children's requests can cause confusion for many children.

INCORRECT INFORMATION

Adults confuse children by not correcting them when they make a mistake or get information wrong. A young boy at my school lived with his mother, but spent much time at his grandmother's house. He developed the habit of calling his grandmother by the name of "mother." It was apparent that his family had not corrected him or explained the difference to him. The child would come to school and call "mother" as he addressed his grandmother. When the woman picked him up, the other children in the class would ask, "Is that your mother?" The older woman would then reply, "No, I'm his grandmother." This young boy was bright and intelligent. He knew his colors, numbers, letters, and information in school that left the other children in class far behind him. I really believe that the child had earlier called his grandmother, "mother," and he was never corrected for calling her by that name. As a result, he learned the information wrong and reteaching the correct way to address his grandmother was a slow process. If adults turn their heads and ignore when children make errors, children will assume that what they have said is right and acceptable.

Children become confused by the inconsistency in adult's stories and information. A little girl in my class came and told me that she had a new brother. I knew her mother was not pregnant so I asked the mother about the girl's statement. The mother explained that the boy was her cousin and that he was staying with the family temporarily. Later that week, I saw the girl's grandmother with the little boy and she told me that the boy was the brother to the little girl in my class. It was obvious that I was hearing two stories about this child's place in the family. I can certainly understand why the girl was confused whether this little boy was her cousin or her brother. She had heard her grandmother telling her that the boy was her brother and her mother telling her the boy was her cousin. The little girl was not intentionally lying about the little boy being her brother. She was confused because she had heard different information about who the little boy was from two important people in her life. When examining a story a child tells, an observer must listen for consistency in the story.

Children sometimes become very frustrated because they become confused by something the parent told them and something the teacher tells them. A child may be so sincere, but totally misunderstand a situation. Micah brought his valentines to school in a decorated bag. His mom had told him to keep the valentines in the bag on the way to school so he would not lose them. When Micah arrived at school, I took him over to the beautiful decorated bags of the students in the class and asked him to put the valentines in the bags. I started to help him pass out the valentines to the correct child's bag. Micah started to cry, "My mom told me to keep the valentines in this bag." He did not understand sharing the valentines with others. They were his valentines and he had made them for himself. A few hours later Micah saw the other children passing out their valentines and then he asked me if he could hand out his valentines. I have seen this happen at other times when a young child buys a birthday present for another child and then wants to keep the present for him or her self. Children may assume that the present is for themselves rather than a gift to someone else.

Sometimes children become confused by the lack of information that adults give them. A young boy came to my class on day and told me that he was sleeping over at this cousin's house. He was so excited about the upcoming visit that he repeated it several times that day. He kept telling the class, "I am going over to my cousin's house at four o'clock and I am walking there all by myself." As a teacher, I warned the little boy that it would be much safer for his parents to take him to his cousin's house or to walk there with a group of friends. Each time he told the story the would emphasize, "I am walking to my cousin's house at four o'clock all by myself." He assured me several times that he could make it to his cousin's house all by himself. His father came to pick him up later that day. I commented to dad how excited the boy was that he was going to walk to his cousin's house. The father looked at the boy and said, "You thought you were going to walk to your cousin's house all by yourself?" The boy responded, "yes." The father then clarified to the boy that he would drive him to his cousin's house. The child had not received enough information about how he was getting to his cousin's house so he made up his story.

FEELINGS AND EMOTIONS

A child's request or story may become more intense as the child figures out the emotional level of the parent or adult. The adult can confuse the child by being angry at him or her one minute and then feeling sorry for the child a few minutes later. I saw a father at the park get angry at his son and give him a spanking. Five minutes later the father felt bad about spanking the boy. The father went over and hugged the boy and gave him a dollar. The little boy learned that he was rewarded when his father was angry with him. The child may want more money the next time a similar incident occurs in his life. For example, after another incident the little boy may not settle for a dollar from his father. The child may want five dollars from his father and then he will promise to behave better. The child has leaned that he can manipulate his father. It is not difficult for a child to learn the emotional weaknesses of parents and adults. Issues of power and control can be key factors in the stories that some children tell. To achieve their goal of getting their way, children may lie, manipulate, threaten, and change their version of a story. Adults must examine what the child's motive is in telling the story. Knowing the motives and reasons why a child is telling the story helps in getting a clear picture of the type of child who makes up a story.

Adults do not always understand how children really feel about them. An adult may become horrified to think that a child is talking to a police officer or social worker about him or her. It is hard to read how a child feels about a parent, teacher or day care worker. As a teacher in the public schools, there was a little boy in my class who was in trouble almost every day. He would constantly get his name on the board, sit in time out, or get a note home. I was certain that the little boy did not like me as his teacher. However, when I talked with his mother at a parent conference she informed me that he loved me as a teacher and that he really liked my class. I was shocked because I figured the child probably resented me for staying after him about his inappropriate classroom behavior. Although I was firm about the classroom rules with the child, there was still a sense of respect.

Children become confused because they do not know the purpose of the things that adults ask them to do. An elementary student was complaining at church one Sunday that he did not want to go on a camping trip that his grandmother insisted that he go to for the weekend. An older man at the church provided an excellent sounding board for the boy as he gave all of the reasons why he did not want to go on the trip. The boy gave excuses like, "The trip will be stupid; My grandmother is making me go to the silly mountain; and I do not want to go on this dumb camping trip." The older gentleman kept coming back with more positive responses like, "Go and enjoy breathing the fresh mountain air; Give it a try; You may really enjoy yourself; and You will enjoy yourself because you will not be around your grandmother." The boy soon realized that there was a purpose in going on the trip, although he had it in his mind that it was the worse possible experience.

A child may become very confused by something that happens in an adult household or a community situation. Because a child is so self-centered in his or her world, the child may think every situation relates directly back to him or her. Children become confused when they hear their parents arguing or having a fight. They do not understand that the parents may be venting steam from a stressful day at work or planning a big event with many details. Children relate to their world and when they fight or disagree with friends they say, "I hate you," or "You are not my friend anymore." They remember a friend breaking their favorite toy or pushing them down on the ground and hurting their knee. The child becomes confused watching mom and dad, two people the child loves, fighting and bad-mouthing each other. Children do not understand an adult couple debating an issue, looking at two points of view, and examining their emotions and feelings about life decisions. They may have difficulty watching their parents fight and cry. The elements of forgiveness, cooling off, and calming down after the argument may be difficult for the child to understand.

The child can take the parent's or adult's distress very serious and personal. A child may even feel guilty that something bad happened in the family and blames himself or herself for the disaster. Take for example, a young girl who wants an expensive bedroom set that her parents can not really afford. She hears her parents arguing about how they would pay for the furniture. Dad wants to put it on the credit card and mom says, "We can not afford it." The fight continues for hours and the girl realizes that she can really live without the bedroom furniture.

The next day, her parents tell her they are separating or moving out of the house. The girl feels guilty that she has caused the break-up of her parents over the bedroom furniture. She does not realize the other factors involved in the marital relationship. This type of guilt in children's stories is heard after major disasters. A child remembers that he or she was bad or did something wrong the day before a big tornado or hurricane. The child may begin to think that he or she caused the entire incident to happen. A major destruction of the families home puts stress on children and they need reassurance from adults that it was not their fault. Adults can confuse children with a busy, fast paced, stressed lifestyle. They may not even realize that some of the things they say confuse the mind of a child and cause them to distort information.

CHAPTER SIX

COVER UP OR DISTRACT A WRONG

When children make up a story or tell a fib, they are often just trying to avoid getting into trouble and they want to cover up and distract from a wrong they have committed. I had a little boy about the age of five years old in my class. He was smart and adventurous. I knew by observing him in class that he was always looking to discover things. The boy really enjoyed being outdoors and finding things in the natural environment. One afternoon at school, his mother approached me to show me a huge bruise on his ankle. She told me that her son had told her that he had hurt it on the playground. I told the mother that he never cried or told me about hurting his ankle on the playground. Later that day, I questioned and talked to the boy about how he hurt his ankle. The child told me that he had hurt his ankle while riding on his bike. That explanation made perfect sense to me because the bruise could have easily come from bumping his ankle against the bicycle pedal or kick stand. To this day, I really believe that the boy was trying to cover up the fact that he was riding the bike when his mother had told him not to ride it. After he hurt his ankle, he rationalized to his mother that he hurt it at school so he would not get in trouble at home. The child told a lie to avoid getting in trouble and had a different version of the story for the teacher and the parent.

Some parents really try to help their children get to the bottom or the truth about a situation. One day we did play dough activities in our class and one of the teacher's daughters stuck a can of playdough in her backpack and took it home. The parent confronted her daughter about the playdough. The daughter said, "The teacher gave it to me." The mother had her daughter bring the playdough back to me the following morning. We had a discussion and the parent and student understood that I had not given the students playdough to take home. I thanked the student for being honest and bringing back the playdough to school. The daughter had made up a story to cover up her wrong, but the parent helped her clarify the details and understand that it was the wrong thing to do.

Sometimes a child is unwilling to admit that he or she made a mistake so that fault is blamed on someone else. Students picked up their jackets each day as they left class. Keon accidentally picked up the wrong jacket and took it home. The next day he walked into class and told my teacher's aide, Mrs. Kyle, she had given him the wrong coat. He refused at all costs to take any responsibility for taking the wrong jacket home. Keon might have thought he was going to get in serious trouble for taking the jacket or simply did not know how to explain that he made a mistake. By blaming someone else for his mistake, he was able to cover up and distract from his wrong.

EMBARRASSMENT AND BLAME

A child's embarrassment about an incident may determine with whom the child shares the story. For example, I had a young girl in my class who apparently had stepped on something stinky in the playground. Amy kept going over by the sink to get paper towels to clean her shoe. When I asked Amy what happened, she just smiled. I assumed she must have stepped on something stinky, and when I asked her a second time she just smiled and kept cleaning her shoe. The class returned to the carpet for storytime during the transition period. Amy then shared what really happened with Mark. It was not long before Mark shouted out that Amy stepped on "dog poop" during recess. Amy chose not to share that information with her teacher for several reasons. She was embarrassed by the smell and upset by the disgusting incident that happened to her. Amy's decision not to answer could be based on thinking she might get into trouble for being messy. Amy was a student who never went to time out and strived to do her best. By not answering the question Amy was able to cover up and distract from her mistake even though it was not that serious.

The same incident can happen in a classroom between two children and each will have a different version of the story. Two children were fighting over a toy and the teacher separated the two children. They were each given a toy, but had to play alone. One child went home and told her mother that, "She was a bad girl." The other child went home and told her mother that, "The teacher was mean to her." This parent showed up at school accusing the teacher of being mean to her daughter. Once the teacher explained that the child was fighting over the toy, the parent understood that the child was not as innocent as she had convinced her mother. The easy way out for the child was to blame the whole incident on the teacher to cover up her wrong. This put the teacher in an uncomfortable situation of having to explain her actions because the child made up an accusation. The child did not realize she could have hurt the teacher's reputation by falsely blaming the incident on her.

If a child makes up a story to cover his or her wrong, it is frequently done so the child will look good to others. Some children do this so that they can look perfect in the eyes of their parents, relatives, teachers, or friends. It is so much easier to criticize and accuse someone else of something than to admit a fault or mistake. One day as I observed my students during recess, I found the students trying to pin their unhappiness on another student. One little girl came running to me crying that Calvin had pushed her down on the ground. Calvin was on the other side of the playground. I had just watched as she slipped on the gravel on the nearby sidewalk and then started to cry. Calvin was a boy who was in trouble often and I noticed that she was just using him to blame her accident on as she ran to tell the teacher on him.

Another little girl came to school with a swollen eye. She never mentioned that on the previous day anyone had hit or bothered her. She arrived at school and her aunt told me that (You guessed it!) Calvin had hit her in the eye. The teacher's aide and I told that aunt that the girl never told us anything. The little girl was in tears after the aunt questioned her and she admitted that she made up the story. No one really knows how the girl hurt her eye, but it was so much easier to blame it on Calvin than to admit the truth. Calvin became the scapegoat as he had to bare the blame for other people's misdeeds and mistakes.

In both of the above cases it was much easier for the girls to blame their accidents and situations on Calvin than to simply admit they hurt themselves. The little girl who slipped on the gravel could have said, "I hurt myself," or "I fell down," instead of, "Calvin pushed me down." She chose to put the blame on someone else. The girl with the swollen eye could have bumped it while playing in her mother's room, which was off limits to her. Instead of admitting the truth or simply telling what really happened, she put the blame on Calvin.

I have also seen children make up a story because they are hurt by the way others treated or wronged them. The child's mechanism for dealing with this pain is to miscommunicate or blame the incident on another person. I took a class of students on a field trip to a clown factory. The class divided into two parts and took turns riding the carousel. While I was on the carousel with half of the class, a parent bought bubble gum for the other half of the class. The action by the parent caused a change of personality in the students. Instead of being happy about the wonderful, beautiful carousel ride, the student's behavior turned to anger, fighting and jealousy on the bus ride home. It was a long ride home and the bus was not going to stop for me to buy bubble gum for the rest of the class. Imagine a child going home to tell his or her mother that the teacher did not buy him or her a piece of bubble gum. The teacher might be blamed for the parent's action on the field trip. A child may become so outraged and angry about not getting a piece of bubble gum that he or she shares the pain by blaming the situation on someone else.

A child may be experiencing a health problem, but think there is something wrong. The child could even blame the condition on another student to avoid getting in trouble. I have heard young children cry about another student hitting them or hurting them, but on closer examination I will find out that the child simply did not know how to describe a health problem. A cute little girl came running up to me one day to say that she hurt her eye and that another student was putting his hands in her eye. Upon closer inspection, I discovered that she had an eyelash in her eye. She did not know how to describe what was wrong with her eye. By blaming the eye problem on another student, she knew that would not get her in trouble and she received help from the teacher to solve the problem. Children who have difficulty explaining what is wrong with them may blame it on someone else to avoid getting in trouble and obtaining help for the problem.

KEEPING SILENT

Some children do not go home from school and tell their parents everything that happened that day in the classroom. Whenever I would correct children and get after them about their negative or unruly behavior, I would wonder what they told their parents. One small girl, who for the most part was very polite and cooperative, was having a very hard time following directions. I kept asking her two or three times to do each task and she was very slow to follow directions and cooperate. I finally took her aside and quietly told her that if she did not start following directions, I would send a note home to her mother. She broke into tears and after a short cry she was wonderful and followed directions perfectly for the rest of the day. A few days later, I felt I owed her mother an explanation about what happened because I was a little unsure what the child might have told her about the incident. The mother said her daughter never mentioned a thing about the classroom incident where she was in trouble. Some children keep quiet and mum because they do not want to get in trouble again when they get home from school. They can become very selective about the information they share between home and school.

My mother has a very strong personality and she would stand up for her children through thick and thin. Whenever I would get in trouble at school (which was rare) I never told my mom about it. At a young age, I kept quiet and did not rock the boat if I was in trouble. The primary reason I was so quiet was that I knew my mother would become furious at the teacher. I did not want to see my teacher be racked over the coals because I was in trouble for a minor incident. I knew I would face the teacher at school each day. To cover up a minor wrong or incident was so much easier than to have it blown out of proportion. Keeping quiet was a better option than causing a major rift between my mother and the teacher. I guess I had observed my mother as she defended my older brothers and sister to their teachers whenever they had been in trouble.

Some children have specific reasons they keep quiet about their wrongs. You cannot totally blame some children for being quiet about their wrongs or trying to cover up an incident. There are some parents that are extremely abusive both verbally and physically if the child gets into trouble at school. There have been times that I have told parents that their children were misbehaving and then I would feel extremely bad for the children when I saw how the parent reacted to the news. One parent reacted by threatening the child and saying, "I am going to whip your butt when we get home." Another little boy had stepped on another child's foot in class and when his mother was told, she went over and stomped on the little boy's foot saying, "How does that feel?" I really felt bad for the child as his two hundred pound mother stepped on his foot and he began to cry. If I know the parent reacts harshly to a child about a minor incident, I often do not share small things the child has done wrong with the parent. I could certainly empathize with these children in covering up a wrong.

INCORRECT DETAILS

A child making up a story to cover a wrong may give incorrect details to a law enforcement officer investigating a crime. A school principal once shared a story with me about an attempted abduction of a student. A young girl was pulled into a car by a stranger, but after she screamed and yelled real loud, the stranger released her. When the child told the police about the incident, she told them that it happened at 3:00 PM, right after school. The principal probably was surprised that no one witnessed the crime since that was the time that school was out and there were lots of school children in the vicinity of the attempted abduction. Finally, after more intense questioning, the girl admitted that she had gone to a nearby recreation center before the incident and that the event took place about 4:00 PM. The girl was trying to cover up the fact that she was forbidden to go to the recreation center, so she changed the time of the incident. Although the attempted abduction occurred, the girl changed an important detail of the time of the incident to cover up a wrong.

To cover up a potential wrong doing, a child may change their version of the story when asked by their parents. They may even correct their parents with the traditional phrase, "I did not say that," or "That's not what I said." For example, a child tells his parents he has a class after school. The parent asks the child what time the class meets. The child responds, "It meets from 5:00 to 9:00 PM." The parent is very suspicious because he knows the class does not meet that long. He calls the school and finds out the class only meets from 5:00 to 6:30 PM The father confronts his son about the time of the class. The son replied that he had not said the class lasted from five to nine o'clock, but rather the class started at five o'clock and the other classes lasted until nine o'clock. The child turns the situation around to confuse the parents and put the blame of the misunderstanding on the parent. The child may have been planning to sneak out with friends but when his plans were discovered by his father, he changed his version to cover up his wrong and stay out of trouble.

Children may intentionally leave details out of a story to avoid any confrontations with their parents. My parents were very strict that I could not date until I was sixteen years old. In elementary school, I attended a Halloween costume party. My mother was in a hurry that night when she dropped me off at the party, so I waved good-bye and ran up to the house as she drove away. The girl having the party had the house ready to have fun and her parents were out of town. There were four girls and four boys at the party. We spent that evening dancing, holding hands and stealing a few kisses behind the shed. When my mother picked me up from the party later that evening, I failed to mention that it was an unsupervised party. I also left out the detail that there were boys at the party, and I certainly did not mention anything about the dancing, holding hands or kissing. I told about eating the food and I knew I would not get in trouble for that part of the story.

Many stories children tell are innocent and they may only want to cover up getting in trouble for something they were doing wrong. A story may be kept a secret for months after an incident has occurred so the impact of the wrong doing is lessened in the parent's eyes. Children may not share stories about the fact they have stolen chewing gum until time has passed. Perhaps a certain topic comes up at a family reunion and an uncle shares a story about stealing something when he was a kid. Suddenly the child tells a story about taking gum from a store. The child has already chewed the pack of gum and the evidence is gone. The youngster is very relieved to get it off his or her chest and a confession has been made. The child does not worry so much about getting into trouble because the incident has happened so long ago. The child may have shared the story with their friends at a slumber party or selected relatives. There are children who fear the consequences of their actions so they become very secretive about what they share and with whom they talk.

To distract from a wrong, a child may change a story to avoid getting in trouble. Take for example, children playing on a large school playground. The children are warned specifically not to play on the monkey bars because they are too young. A young boy does not obey his teacher and falls off the monkey bars and scratches his knee. He comes running to the teacher and does not tell him or her that he fell off the monkey bars. Instead, the child tells the teacher that he fell down on the ground. He knows that he does not want to get in trouble again for something prohibited on the playground. The child gets his needs met as the teacher puts a bandaid on his knee and avoids being sent to time out for disobeying the playground rules. Children may change the version of the story at home, school, day care centers, or at play to avoid facing the truth they were doing something wrong or in a prohibited place.

REVENGE AND EXCUSES

Revenge is used by children as motives for making up stories. They have a tremendous desire to get back at a person who has wronged or hurt them. A child named Jimmy loses or gets his snack money stolen at school. He assumes he knows who took the money, even though there is no evidence to prove it. Jimmy makes up a story that a boy named Gary took the money and had pestered him all day. The teacher then questions innocent Gary about the accusations that Jimmy has made against him. This type of revenge is an intentional act to hurt or humiliate another person. Jimmy has become very vindictive and is trying to justify the wrong that happened to him, by punishing Gary and using him as the scapegoat. Instead of admitting that he lost the money or left it on the lunch table where someone took it, Jimmy decides to blame his mistake, or wrong on someone else.

Jimmy's choice to make up a story against Gary shows that he is revengeful and wants to impose a penalty on another person. Professionals and parents must not overlook the motives of revenge and anger a child may be expressing toward another person in his or her stories.

Revenge can become a source of power for some children. I observed a young elementary child who seemed to have manipulated the school he was in and became quite a powerful person. The boy was in trouble numerous times and was well known for telling stories and making up far-fetched incidents. One day he decided to turn on his teacher, so he told the assistant principal that the teacher hit him. Of course there were no other witnesses, other than the teacher and the student. Even though this student had a history of trouble and making up stories, it still put the teacher's professionalism on the line. The teacher had to explain the situation to the assistant principal and to the school district police. The student moved to another class and was able to have his way again. It was obvious that the student was revengeful of his teacher so the teacher was the perfect person to target his story and get his way. He was powerful enough to persuade the school administrator to believe his story even though his reputation was far from being squeaky clean.

Some child will make up any excuse to avoid telling the truth. A young boy came to school one morning with red marks all over his hand. When I asked why his hands were red, he responded, "It's blood." I told him I knew it was not blood and I asked him if he was using red magic markers. He said, "It is blood." Upon closer examination, I saw the color red around his mouth. I soon realized that he had been eating some rather red candy. He would never admit eating candy and stuck with his story that, "It was blood." I think he knew that his mother was always after him about eating candy, so to avoid the chance of getting in trouble, he used the "blood" excuse. I finally asked him how he got the blood on his hands and face. He responded, "From the plant" in his yard. The class had been studying a unit on things that grow and planting grass and flowers. He might have fooled some people by saying he scratched his hands on plants although there were no scratch marks. The red stains around his mouth were a sure sign he raided the candy bag.

The child may have to make up a story quickly just to avoid getting in trouble or facing immediate consequences or punishment for something they have done. A child dials 9-1-1 and hangs up the phone quickly. The child does not think he or she has done anything bad even though he or she may have been playing on the phone all afternoon. When the fire station calls to inform the parents and check on the 9-1-1 call, the child must face the consequences. The child quickly tells the parents, "It was an accident." A parent may take the telephone privileges away from the child for a week. Children may try many techniques to avoid getting in trouble for a wrong. Teachers will share hundreds of stories about students who deny they stole something or hit another student when the teacher has caught them red-handed. Students think about their behavior the rest of the day at school or on the bus ride home. By the time the parents arrive home from work, the child had time to think through the details of the story and decide upon which parts of the story are better to share.

Incidents such as these abound in the school environment. A child eats very slowly and at the end of the lunch period she asks the teacher for a second helping of desert. The teacher tells the student, "No, lunch is over for today." The child goes home and tells the parent that the teacher would not give her any food. The next day the teacher is confronted by the parent who is angry about the child's story. The teacher usually calms the parents once they hear a full explanation of the situation.

Similarly, some students are just very picky eaters. They will turn down food and refuse to eat it when offered to them. These students will go home and their parents will ask them what they ate for lunch. I have heard stories from teachers where students will go home from school and tell their parents that the cafeteria workers or teachers would not allow them to eat or select food. These students are often questioned strongly before they admit the truth about what happened in the cafeteria or at school. Covering up or distracting from a wrong is probably one of the most common reasons that children make up stories. Most children do not want to get into trouble, so a story is quickly made up in order to avoid punishment or a reprimand.

CHAPTER SEVEN

CONCERNS AND CAUTIONS IN EXAMINING CHILDREN'S STORIES

Professionals and parents who examine children's stories must use caution and concern to decide if the story is fabricated or true. This is not always a simple decision and can easily be considered as a "gray area." Professionals may find they simply do not have enough information to make an important decision about the reality of a child's story. Another meeting or encounter with the child may reveal that he or she has totally changed the story and forgot the entire incident. The child's answers to questions are often times influenced by peers or family members. The child may also be confused by the adult's questions or unable to explain his or her answer because of limited life experiences, covering up a wrong, or vocabulary. The stories children tell must be looked at from within the child's perspective and social environment. In the following pages I have developed one hundred cautions to consider when examining whether the child has made up the story or whether it could be reality. These are cautions for professionals and parents to examine before drawing conclusions about children's stories.

100 CAUTIONS IN EXAMINING CHILDREN'S STORIES

1. Changes in the child's living conditions may alter the child's stories.
2. A strong influence in the child's life may persuade him or her to change the story.

3. The child could be telling a story because of peer pressure.

4. Family influence may put stress on the child to give a one-sided story.

5. Children may not tell the truth because they are afraid of getting in trouble.

6. The child may have made up the story from a television show or movie.

7. Perhaps, the child just enjoys telling far-fetched, imaginative and creative stories.

8. Listen to the vocabulary a child uses to explain the story to see if he or she is accurately describing what really happened.

9. Be cautious in believing everything a child says.

10. The child may be getting much attention and affection for making up the story.

11. Lack of real life experiences may be the reason the child really does not understand the story he or she is telling.

12. Negative experiences may have distorted the child's sense of reality.

13. The child may be repeating someone else's story.

14. The child may be imitating a behavior or experience that happened to someone else.

15. Seek to find out if what happened to the child was an accident or on purpose.

16. Is the child trying to purposely hurt, bother, or have revenge on someone by making up a story?

17. The child may be making up a story to cover his or her wrong doing.

18. Is the child being influenced by a sibling to say something?

19. Did the child fully understand the question?

20. If the child's vocabulary is advanced for a young person, try to find out where he or she learned these words.

21. Try to get the whole picture and listen for half-truths or inconsistencies.

22. Rephrase the questions children do not understand.

23. Is the child really trying to explain a dream in the story?

24. The child may have made up the story to create something or someone to become a part of his or her life.
25. Is the child seeking to impress someone by telling the story?
26. Did the child misinterpret part or all of the story?
27. The child may become confused with the words adults use when in conversation with each other.
28. Ask open ended questions to children to get more information.
29. Avoid the use of yes or no questions that give only limited information.
30. Is the child blaming an incident on someone else to avoid admitting a mistake?
31. Observe to see if the child is simply imitating or following a parent's example.
32. Does it build the child's self-esteem to tell the story?
33. Try to find out if the child has a habit of making up stories or telling lies.
34. Is the child agreeing and answering yes to many questions to avoid getting in trouble?
35. The child may be trying to avoid confrontation or a scene by making up the story.
36. The child may be embarrassed to discuss the real story so he or she makes up another story.
37. Is the child making up the story to avoid being punished?
38. Children may be dealing with a conflict and the story is just a way to get attention so that they can get help for a deeper problem.
39. The child may be mad at someone and makes up a story for revenge.
40. Is the child willingly agreeing with friends and siblings without expressing his or her own viewpoint?
41. Could a family member be coaching the child to answer questions a certain way?
42. Is the child trying to agitate or imitate someone by making up the story?
43. Are the characters in the child's story believable or contrived?

44. Analyze the tone of voice the child is using to tell and communicate the story.

45. Observe the eye contact and gestures the child uses when expressing the story.

46. Try to help the child stick to the point of the story if he or she gets off track.

47. Listen in the story to understand if the child is blaming or accusing someone to shift the responsibility of an action.

48. Keep questions to children brief and short.

49. Observe if the child is paying attention to the question or focusing in on something else in the room.

50. What are the circumstances and events that lead up to the child sharing the story?

51. Is there any real evidence of wrongdoing from the child's story?

52. Are the details of the child's story clear?

53. Was the child a victim of circumstance as he or she describes the story?

54. Clarify for yourself if the child was a participant or just an observer of the situation.

55. Consider questioning the child alone since parents and siblings often make comments that influence the child's answers.

56. A combination of events may have influenced the child's answers or stories.

57. The child may be afraid to answer questions from someone in a uniform or who carries a gun.

58. Is the child just gossiping a story he or she heard at school or in the family?

59. Follow up on jokes or off the cuff remarks to make sure there are not more serious issues.

60. Keep all questions, comments, and remarks simple and at the child's level.

61. In conducting an interview with a child try to make sure that he or she feels comfortable and relaxed.

62. Does the child exhibit any awkward or unusual behaviors while telling the story to indicate other health or behavioral problems?

63. Is the child's story consistent or do the details of the story change?

64. Get enough information so that the child relates the entire story without hiding important details or facts.

65. Consider if the child is trying to protect or shield another family member or friend in the story.

66. Does the child seem uncertain or unsure of the story?

67. Did the child's story raise doubts or new questions?

68. Observe if the child's story seems to ramble or go off aimlessly in many directions.

69. Is the child sharing a story naturally or just reciting a prepared story or speech?

70. If unclear on the details of the story, consider talking with the child a second time.

71. Schedule a time when the child is fully awake and not sleepy to ask a series of questions.

72. Two people talking with a child may get two stories; so look for consistencies and inconsistencies.

73. Did the child's account of the incident provide information about other problems or concerns?

74. Is the child a reliable and dependable source of information?

75. Consider if the child telling the story is under a stressful home environment such as a divorce situation or loss of a significant family member.

76. What is the maturity level of the child telling the story?

77. Collect and examine the facts of the story, understanding that children may include some silly, frivolous or unusual ideas in the story.

78. Sometimes children mumble, so encourage them to speak loudly and clearly when telling you the story.

79. Ask more questions if the child starts to babble to see if the child is coherent and understandable.

80. If the child refused or is unwilling to talk with you, reschedule a different time for the interview because the child may be sick or tired.

81. Is the child serious and sincere about the story or is it just a big joke or wise crack?

82. Could the child make up a story out of boredom or for thrill and excitement?

83. The story the child created may be from a book or computer program.

84. Is the child trying to make a big fuss to get attention from the story?

85. Can the child explain the story so it makes sense?

86. Are there mistakes or doubts that keep reoccurring in the child's story?

87. Does the child waver and change his or her answers after each question?

88. Props such as puppets or dolls may help a timid or shy child open up more with his or her thoughts and feeling.

89. Is the child fretting, whining and complaining in the story to get his or her way?

90. Does the child sound confident and sure of his or her story?

91. Is the child adding irrelevant details to create excitement to the story?

92. Does the child telling the story have a major crisis in his or her life?

93. Is the child's story meant to criticize, blame or hurt another person?

94. Are there cultural elements in a child's story the interviewer or investigator may not understand?

95. Does the story reveal important information about the child's routines, habits, and customs?

96. Do elements of the child's story reveal a dishonesty, betrayal or insincere attitude?

97. Is the child's story a willful and deliberate plan to hurt someone?

98. Listen closely to see if the child unveils, identifies and shares relevant information in his or her story.

99. Does the child take any responsibility for his or her actions in the story or is the entire incident blamed on other people?

100. Be honest, collect much information, and keep a watchful eye on the way a child tells a story before passing judgment, thereby avoiding a decision that can change a child's or adult's life forever.

CONCERNS IN QUESTIONING THE CHILD'S STORY

There are several concerns to consider when examining whether the child may be telling the truth.

1) SPECIFIC DETAILS IN THE STORY

A key point to consider is how descriptive and specific the details are in the child's story. Some children are vague and unclear on details, while other children give very specific details when describing what has happened to them. Pay special attention to what a child is trying is communicate. One child may say, "He touched me," but does not give any definite information other than a brief statement. The statement may seem very vague from a young child who touches and hugs many people. However, a child may say, "He touched me," but without any probing goes on to describe where he or she was touched. This is a clear signal that the child may know what is happening and further questioning is needed to verify whether this information is true. The concern to consider is whether the child gives specific details in the story or indefinite, general and vague accounts that cause doubt.

2) THE CHARACTERS IN THE STORY

When the child tells the story, listen as he or she describes the people and events in the story. Are people really involved in the child's life or are they make believe? When a young girl tells me about a birthday party at Aunt Patty's house, it might sound believable. Once I discussed it with the mother, I found there was not an

Aunt Patty or a birthday party. Please note that in extremely rare cases an adult may give a child a false or fictitious name to seek the child's secrecy about abuse or mistreatment.

When a child constantly tells a story about Uncle Dan at the beach and you discover there is an Uncle Dan, then you know the character is perhaps true and real. You still need to question the child further to find out if the story about this real person or event is true.

3) OBSERVE THE CHILD'S MANNERISMS AND HABITS

Watch as the child tells the story to see if he or she has any unusual mannerisms, characteristics, or habits that show if his or her character is reliable and sincere in telling the story. I taught a student who lied throughout the school year. I observed him telling lies to get himself out of trouble or to make trouble. Trevor would answer questions opposite of the truth. Ronald McDonald visited my classroom and gave all the children a package of cookies. Before Ronald left, I asked the class if everyone had cookies and they all said, "yes," except Trevor. He was hiding his package of cookies in the back of his chair. I gave him my package of cookies, but several minutes later another student yelled, "Trevor has two packages of cookies." That incident was just the beginning of a long series of untruths Trevor would share with the class. Because of Trevor's constant lying, I would question almost any story he told with great skepticism. If professionals find that a child required numerous parent conferences at school for lying, stealing or cheating, it raises the question of his or her truthfulness and honesty about the situation.

Trevor's stories continued to have an impact on his academic progress. During a math activity, Trevor would shout out the correct answer to every math question. When asked to complete a math assignment on paper, Trevor would mark each answer incorrectly and say, "I cannot do it." Trevor did the assignment two more times and kept marking the wrong answers. As a reward and incentive, the students completing the assignment correctly were given gummy worms to eat. Finally, Trevor was warned that if he did not finish the math assignment, he would not get a gummy worm. Knowing that he was not going to get a gummy worm, he did the assignment one more time and answered all the questions correctly. Children in school sometimes develop bad habits and play games with the teachers and administrators. I have observed cases where children are taken to the office to discuss failing grades. A student once said, "I made straight A's at my other school and this is just a bad teacher at this school." On closer examination of the student's previous school records, it was discovered he was also failing courses there. His story sounded believable, but the school records gave a different picture of the situation.

As a teacher, I have observed children that also have extremely honest and dependable personalities. One young girl in my class was Candy and her whole attitude about life was to do the right thing. If I needed a clear picture about a class problem between two children, I knew I could depend on Candy's answer to be the truthful version. The behavior I observed in Candy was very responsible, so I would know she provided a much more credible story. Please note, that is not to say that the more credible and responsible child is necessarily telling the truth. It just means the character of the child may be one that exhibits honesty more often than an irresponsible child. Further questioning is needed to verify other concerns and information about the story.

4) INTERFERENCE FROM OTHERS

To get a better picture of whether a child is telling the truth, try to ask questions when the child is alone. I have seen numerous times where peers, siblings, parents, and the other relatives have interfered as the child is answering questions. It is not uncommon for a child to look at a parent if he or she does not know how to answer the question. The interference can be both verbal or nonverbal. The police officer asks something and notices the child looking at the mother who is giving a disapproving glance. Answers that children give to questions may change if children believe they may be in trouble for something.

Sometimes other people will interrupt the child as he or she tries to answer the question. I ask a child a series of questions from a checklist before he is enrolled in a pre-kindergarten class. The parent was on the other side of the classroom filling out some additional paperwork for the child, but she was listening as I asked the child the questions. Each time I asked the child to tell me something, the parent would correct the child's answer. I had to constantly request the parent not to provide answers for the child. As a result, I asked the parent to complete paperwork in an adjoining room so the child could answer the questions.

Some young children and siblings want to help their brothers, sisters, or friends with a difficult situation. They feel sorry for each other and will tell another child what to say so the child will not get in trouble. This is a strong and powerful force that can be very persuasive when a child is telling about a situation. A child may change or modify an original story at the persistence of another significant person in the child's life. A minor problem for the child may develop into a major situation because of interference from others. Interference from others puts a large amount of pressure on children and could force them to change a story unwillingly.

5) LISTEN FOR RELEVANT INFORMATION

Not every child tells the same story the same way. Adults may tell a story in a logical sequence with precise details and information. A child may share bits and pieces of a story at different times. The child might only reveal what is on the forefront of his or her thoughts on that particular day. If the child is interviewed the next day, he or she may share totally different information. The child may be influenced by someone to change the story. In observing children, I try to listen for relevant and consistent information. Some details change in the child's story, while other descriptions of events or people remain constant and unchanging. Keep in mind the child is getting attention from the person questioning him or her and this may cause the child to fabricate information so the story is exciting and wonderful for the listener.

A child's frustrations on a particular day could influence the way he or she tells a story and the kind of information the story reveals. For example, a child observes her parents having an argument. The father leaves the house and slams the door. The mother might start crying and the child might respond by sitting on the mother's lap. Although, the child loves both mom and dad, on the that particular day the child is more empathic to the needs of mother. The version of the child's story might be slanted toward the mother and may give the impression that dad is the bad guy. If you question the child about the incident after she has spent the day eating ice cream and going to the park with dad, you might hear a different version of the story. The child could still share relevant and consistent information in the story, but his or her perspective on who was the bad person in the story has shifted.

6) THE CHILD'S SENSE OF REALITY

When listening to a child's account of the story, try to get a sense of the child's realm of reality. Some young children have a good sense of the real world, while other children live in a total fantasy land. I asked my students, "What they wanted to be when they grow up to be an adult?" Over the years I have heard a variety of responses to that question and some of the answers are very realistic, while other responses from the children are in an imaginary world. Realistic responses have included comments like, "I want to be a doctor, teacher, preacher, librarian, ambulance driver, fire fighter, and police officer." On the other hand, children have told me they wanted to be, "dogs, puppies, caterpillars, horses" and a variety of other animals when they grow older. Sometimes the child responds with an idea read from a story or seen on a television show. Students often tell the teacher they want to be spiderman, batman, power rangers, barbie dolls or other cartoon characters seen on television programs.

There was a four year old child in my class several years ago who behaved like a two year old. He would wet his pants, crawl under the table, throw temper tantrums, and even talk like a baby. My observations of the child lead me to see him as extremely immature and confused about his own reality. His mother disagreed with me. She thought her little boy was perfectly logical and would never say anything that was not the absolute truth. I was continually confronting accusations over little comments the child made up about things that happened in the class. My experience over years of teaching in the public schools has been that I seldom have to answer questions or explain situations to parents who have children with a good sense of reality. The majority of time I have answered parent concerns regarding severe behavioral problems by making a recommendation for testing to a special education program. I always shake my head in amazement that I am answering accusations from children who often need counseling, therapy, and special assistance, but whose parents are in a state of denial about the child's problems. When examining a child's sense of reality, a professional may consider many factors. Is the child hiding information because he or she is scared of something or has been threatened by someone? In some cases a child may have a learning disability or problems at school that prevent him or her from accurately communicating a story. There may be a variety of mental health issues that comprise a child's story. For instance, the child may have phobias, anxiety disorders, mood swings, bouts of depression, attention disorders or behavioral problems. The child may be under large amounts of stress from a family situation. There are many factors that may cloud a child's sense of reality. These factors may be unknown because young children are not diagnosed or tested for learning disorders. The person being accused of an untrue incident may be the first to discover that a child truly needs help with his or her problem. Unfortunately, the person being accused also has to answer questions and defend him or her self with the falsehood. These complicated situations need to be explored thoroughly rather than quickly and hastily.

CHAPTER EIGHT

USING QUESTIONING TECHNIQUES WITH CHILDREN

Professionals working with children use questioning techniques for obtaining a variety of information. The reasons behind asking questions can be varied according to the information the professional is trying to obtain.

TEN REASONS PROFESSIONALS USE QUESTIONS WITH CHILDREN

1. TO HELP A CHILD BECOME MORE RESPONSIVE
2. TO STIMULATE A CHILD'S MEMORY
3. TO HIGHLIGHT KEY POINTS OF AN INCIDENT
4. TO HELP EXPLAIN MISUNDERSTANDINGS
5. TO HAVE THE CHILD TELL OR REPHRASE AN INCIDENT
6. TO HELP THE CHILD PUT EVENTS IN ORDER
7. TO FIND HOW PERSONALLY INVOLVED THE CHILD IS IN THE INCIDENT
8. TO SEE IF THE CHILD CHANGES THE STORY
9. TO OBSERVE THE CHILD'S POINT OF VIEW
10. TO DETERMINE HOW THE INCIDENT IMPACTS THE CHIILD'S LIFE

The following pages will include an exploration of some of the issues for professionals who question children.

TO HELP A CHILD BECOME MORE RESPONSIVE

PROS

Using questions to help a child become more responsive can be an effective way to assist the child. Here are some of the benefits of using responsive questions:

⇒ **getting a reaction from a shy child.**

⇒ **giving the child a time to reflect on the story or situation.**

⇒ **observing a child's attitude and temperament in answering the questions.**

⇒ **finding out what type of questions that children respond more openly with a greater comfort level.**

CONS

There are some children who may not react as positively to responsive questions. Some children may:

⇒ **not have the temperament or personality to be open about their lives.**

⇒ **find it painful to be responsive to someone they do not know well.**

⇒ **start to use backlash or revenge against someone who has previously offended or hurt them.**

⇒ **have poor recognition skills to recall information from previous stories.**

TO STIMULATE A CHILD'S MEMORY

PROS

Questions geared to specifically stimulate a child's memory can be helpful in understanding a child's story. The child might be able:

⇒ **to recall important details of an incident.**

⇒ **reminisce an experience that helps to better explain the story.**

⇒ **describe the circumstances leading up to an incident.**

⇒ **share a visual picture of the story.**

CONS

Sometimes questions to stimulate a child's memory may be problematic. The child may:

⇒ **remember a bad or unpleasant experience in his or her life.**

⇒ **recollect an incident that is not related to the story that he or she is being asked specific questions.**

⇒ **recall an experience which he or she has been confused about the details.**

⇒ **repeat a story that someone else has told him or her and make it sound as if it is his or her own story.**

TO HIGHLIGHT KEY POINTS OF AN INCIDENT

PROS

Questions can be used to highlight the key points of an incident. They are beneficial because they help:

⇒ **focus in on the key issues of an incident.**

⇒ **the child see the important points in the story.**

⇒ **bring out pertinent information about the story, incident or situation.**

⇒ **point out what the purpose or meaning is behind the story.**

CONS

Questions that highlight only the key points may be confusing to some children. There can be problems if the child:

⇒ **leaves out small, but important details in a story or case.**

⇒ **emphasizes what he or she thinks is important, but the professional considers them minor and unimportant details.**

⇒ **does not really understand what the professional is asking him or her to describe.**

⇒ **shares numerous irrelevant points and information during the interview.**

TO HELP EXPLAIN MISUNDERSTANDINGS

PROS

Questions are often necessary to help explain misunderstandings. The professional questions the child to help clarify misunderstandings and let the child explain his or her understanding the situation. They allow the child to:

⇒ **tell his or her side of the story.**

⇒ **express concerns or problems that specifically bothered him or her.**

⇒ **clarify misleading information.**

⇒ **admit mistakes or poor decisions.**

CONS

There are some cautions when using questions to explain misunderstandings. The child may:

⇒ **misconceive the information the professional is asking him or her.**

⇒ **have the wrong impression of the whole situation.**

⇒ **feel he or she is going to get into trouble if too much is said during the interview.**

⇒ **not want to go into as many details as the professional wants him or her to share in the interview.**

TO HAVE THE CHILD TELL OR REPHRASE AN INCIDENT

PROS

Questions used appropriately with children may enable them to tell or rephrase an incident. They help children by:

⇒ **allowing them an opportunity to be open about the details of the story.**

⇒ **giving them time to express themselves and their feelings.**

⇒ **letting them clarify unclear details in the story.**

⇒ **allowing them to tell the story from a child's perspective or focus.**

CONS

There can some uncertainties in using questions to help children tell and rephrase stories. Children could respond by:

⇒ **repeating the words of the professional who is asking them questions.**

⇒ **telling a story that someone else has told them.**

⇒ **telling the story and then rephrasing it in a totally different way.**

⇒ **getting off the subject and emphasizing nonessential points.**

TO HELP THE CHILD PUT EVENTS IN ORDER

PROS

Questions may be focused toward helping the child put events in order. These questions are beneficial for the child to:

⇒ **sequence the events in the story.**

⇒ **tell of events or circumstances that occurred prior to the story.**

⇒ **share important details that give a greater understanding of the story.**

⇒ **trace the route or path the child took on a particular day.**

CONS

There can be a few disadvantages of asking the child to put the events in an ordered format. The child may:

⇒ **leave out an important event in the story.**

⇒ **start with the ending of the story and have difficulty looking backward.**

⇒ **remember some events and leave other events out of the story.**

⇒ **not have the sequencing skills to put the story in order.**

TO FIND HOW PERSONALLY INVOLVED THE CHILD IS IN THE INCIDENT

PROS

Questions to find how personally involved children are in the stories and incidents they tell may be very important to professionals. The benefits of this type of questioning include:

⇒ **examining the child's role in the story.**

⇒ **observing how the child views him or her self in relation to others.**

⇒ **seeing how the child looks at other people in his or her life at home, school and other social situations.**

⇒ **paying attention to the depth of the child's involvement in the story.**

CONS

Some of the difficulties in trying to interpret how personally involved children are in a story may include the following:

⇒ **the children may actually be describing themselves in a dream, rather than a true situation.**

⇒ **the children could be characterizing themselves in an incident they saw on television or in a movie.**

⇒ **the children's portrayal of themselves in the story may not be accurate.**

⇒ **some children do not want to talk about themselves.**

TO SEE IF THE CHILD CHANGES THE STORY

PROS

Questions can help provide information on the consistency of the child's story. The professional can observe if the children:

⇒ **tell the story a similar way as he or she asks them a series of questions.**

⇒ **seem to express far-fetched or bizarre ideas in the story.**

⇒ **use vocabulary words that they do not really understand.**

⇒ **bring imaginary characters into their stories.**

CONS

This pattern of questioning can also be difficult for some children. There may be questions that:

⇒ **are confusing to children.**

⇒ **are too complicated for children to understand.**

⇒ **mislead children to innocently change their stories.**

⇒ **shift the child's thinking to a new topic.**

TO OBSERVE THE CHILD'S POINT OF VIEW

PROS

Questions can be utilized for the professional to observe the point of view of the child. This type of questioning may reveal:

⇒ **if children are angry or unhappy about something else in their lives.**

⇒ **if a child has a strong bias or prejudice about something in his or her life.**

⇒ **if the child lacks information to make well thought out decisions.**

⇒ **that children need to come to an understanding of their position in relationship to the real world.**

CONS

Some cautions must be exercised when questioning a child related to his or her point of view. The professional must be cautious not to:

⇒ **make assumptions about what the child is going to say prior to the interview.**

⇒ **draw conclusion before children have shared the points of view.**

⇒ **give ideas to influence the child's point of view.**

⇒ **force children into quick responses and give them time to reflect and share their points of view.**

TO DETERMINE HOW THE INCIDENT IMPACTS THE CHILD'S LIFE

PROS

Professionals may want to get a good idea of how an incident impacts the child's life. Questioning along this line can provide:

⇒ **a sense of the child's innocence.**

⇒ **information on whether the child was harmed emotionally or physically by the story.**

⇒ **a look at how important or nonessential the child views the story or incident.**

⇒ **information on whether the child makes up other stories or incidents on a regular basis.**

CONS

There are some cautions when questioning a child about how an incident may impact his or her life. The professional should be aware that children:

⇒ **sometimes make a minor injury or accident into a big event in their lives.**

⇒ **may be describing an accident that happened to someone else in their life as their own story.**

⇒ **are sometimes dishonest to receive attention or recognition from others.**

⇒ **may make a big scene out of a small incident or occurrence.**

TIPS FOR PROFESSIONALS WHO QUESTION CHILDREN'S STORIES

Here are a few tips to keep in mind when questioning a child:

TIME

Give the child plenty of time to answer the questions. Some children are very shy and introverted and may not answer a question instantly. If they are given enough time to formulate and think about their answer, they may respond after a brief pause.

BUILD TRUST

There are some children who are afraid or do not want to open up to a stranger. They view the professional as a distant person and may not be comfortable sharing their lives. A good idea may be to start the interview with a few light questions to "break the ice" and establish a comfort level with the child.

KEEP THE CHILD ON THE TOPIC

Young children who are growing have a lot of things on their minds. It is not uncommon for children to start talking about one topic and immediately shift to another topic in a matter of seconds. The professional may have to redirect the child back to the topic being discussed.

WATCH THE DETAILS

It is so easy for a professional to give a child too many details before questioning him or her. Sometimes children will just repeat what the adult has already told them. These children really are not answering the questions, but rehashing what the professional has just finished telling them.

BE AWARE OF COMMUNICATION STYLE

Professionals must be aware of verbal and nonverbal communication skills that they are using as they question children. I have noticed that children are very conscious of things life voice tone or eye contact. A professional with a strong, deep voice may want to use a quieter, softer tone with young children.

SETTING FOR THE INTERVIEW

The professional interviewing children must be aware of the setting which he or she is asking the questions. For example, a busy office may be too distracting for the child to focus in on what the professional is asking him or her. Things like phone calls, interruptions, and fax machines may cause children to lose their alertness during the interview.

EVALUATING CHILDREN'S NEEDS RELATED TO THEIR STORIES

A professional trying to help a child must informally evaluate whether the child is making up a story to receive some really help or assistance in his or her life. The following is a list of needs that children may be trying to express from the made-up story:

⇒ **Need for more parent support**

⇒ **Need for someone to listen to their real problems**

⇒ **Need to tell someone they made a mistake**

⇒ **Need to feel important and recognized**

⇒ **Need to feel safe and secure**

⇒ **Need to express themselves to someone other than a family member**

⇒ **Need to receive praise and affection**

⇒ **Need to prove they can do something**

⇒ **Need to search for information and answers to questions**

⇒ **Need affirmation that they are all on the right path**

PROFESSIONALS CAN WORK AS A TEAM TO EVALUATE CHILDREN'S STORIES

The following items are some ideas of how professionals can work together to evaluate children stories:

DEVELOP A TEAM OF PROFESSIONALS FROM DIFFERENT BACKGROUNDS

A team should not be made up of everyone from the same field with similar experiences. For example, a school team made up of teachers would analyze stories from an educational perspective. The team could include school professionals from backgrounds in criminal justice, nursing and psychology with the teachers to analyze the stories with a variety of perspectives.

CONSIDER OTHER FACTORS INVOLVED IN THE INCIDENT OR STORY

A team may want to ask the following types of questions:

Did anyone witness the incident or the child telling the story?

Did any other major events or crises happen to the child prior to the incident?

Was the child angry or disgruntled with anyone prior to the incident?

Does the child have a good understanding of what is going on in his or her immediate environment?

COLLECT ENOUGH INFORMATION TO FULLY UNDERSTAND THE CHILD'S CONCERN

The team may want to analyze the following:

What time of the day did the incident supposedly occur?

Where did the incident happen?

What people were involved in the incident or story?

When adults ask for more specific information they will sometimes find the child does not have a good answer to these questions. Sometimes it becomes obvious that the story is made-up and the child may even confess that the story was not true.

MAKE A LIST OF STRATEGIES THAT COULD HELP THE CHILD

The team could formulate some strategies that could assist the child in the future. These strategies would be based on such things as the background information collected on the child, the severity of the accusation, the credibility of the story and the strength of the child's claim. Professionals could then evaluate the strategies and methods (if any) that could be implemented to help the child in the present and future situations.

KEEPING THE CHILD'S BEST INTEREST

I am a firm believer in keeping the child's best interest at hand. Some children tell the truth and that should be admired as they stand up for what they believe. However, other children are confused, bewildered, and unclear about details of things that happen in their lives. It is our responsibility as adults to help these children stay on track and realize when some of the things they say are silly, jumbled, entangled and in a maze that no one could really interpret. The important thing is that professionals strive to get the best picture they can of the child's situation. I once heard a school counselor mention that she was trained to believe everything a child told her. My perspective is that professionals must be trained to question and examine everything a child tells them to get a clear and true picture of the child's situation. Professionals, who are cautious and examine these stories patiently will be better able to distinguish made-up stories and false accusations that children make from those stories that are true.

BIBLIOGRAPHY

I have listed several books available that would be useful in helping professionals
and parents question and better understand children and the stories they tell.

Aldrich, Sandra P. *Kids Fight When the Phone Rings: And Other Things I Wish
I'd Known When I First Had Children.* Wheaton, IL: Tyndale House
Publishers, 1997.

Brooks, Barbara and Siegel, Paula M. *The Scared Child: Helping Kids Overcome
Traumatic Events.* New York, NY: John Wiley & Sons, 1996

Hallowell, Edward. *When You Worry About the Child You Love.* New York,
NY: Simon & Schuster, 1996.

Ingersoll, Barbara D. and Goldstein, Sam. *Lonely, Sad and Angry: A Parent's
Guide to Depression in Children and Adolescents.* New York, NY:
Doubleday, 1995.

Mason, Diane, Jensen, Gayle and Ryzewicz, Carolyn. *No More Tantrums: A
Parent's Guide to Taming Your Toddler and Keeping Your Cool.* Chicago,
IL: Contemporary Books, 1997.

Novick, Barbara J. and Arnold, Maureen M. *Why Is My Child Having Trouble At
School?* New York, NY: A Jeremy P. Tarcher/Putnam Book, 1995.

Sandoz, Bobbie. *Parachutes for Parents: 12 New Keys to Raising Children for a
Better World.* Chicago, IL: Contemporary Books, 1997.

SUBJECT INDEX

ABOUT THE AUTHOR

Dr. Susan Louise Peterson has a Ph.D. from Oklahoma State University in family relations and child development and a master's degree from the University of Oklahoma in human relations. She has an undergraduate degree from the University of Science & Arts of Oklahoma in sociology with a minor in communications. Susan Louise Peterson has worked professionally as a teacher, college professor and human relations consultant. She is the author of several books in the educational and women's studies areas. In particular, she wrote the book *The Educators' Phrase Book,* as a reference guide to help teachers and students with their educational paperwork.